JUDAISM
in the
Beginning
of
CHRISTIANITY

JUDAISM
in the
Beginning
of
CHRISTIANITY

JACOB NEUSNER

FORTRESS PRESS   PHILADELPHIA

Library of Congress Cataloging in Publication Data

Neusner, Jacob, 1932–
  Judaism in the beginning of Christianity.

  Bibliography: p.
  Includes index.
  1. Judaism—History—Post-exilic period, 586 B.C.
210 A.D. 2. Judaism—Relations—Christianity.
3. Christianity and other religions—Judaism.
4. Hillel, 1st cent. B.C./1st cent. I. Title.
BM177.N475 1984   296'.09   83–48000
ISBN 0-8006-1750-9 (pbk.)

K118083   Printed in the United States of America   1–1750

For
Robert Berchman

TABLE OF CONTENTS

PREFACE

This book addresses the beginning student in the study of New Testament and earliest Christianity. The purpose is to describe the Jewish world of the Land of Israel, into which Jesus was born, in which he lived, and in which, to begin with, his life and teachings took shape and found their original meaning. Since the history of Christianity begins in Israel, the Jewish people, and in Judaism, Israel's religion, students naturally want to know something about that formative context. I hope to serve by describing what seem to me five of the most basic topics. The five chapters then constitute readings for five units generally included in any course syllabus at the beginning of the study of Christianity.

First, we deal with the situation of that country of many names and many peoples, called, by Jews, the Land of Israel, by Romans (not in the first century, to be sure) and by Arabs later on, Palestine, and by Christians from the time of Constantine, "the Holy Land."

Second, we turn to principal types of "Judaism," that is, systems of viewing the world and living life characteristic of distinct groups of Jews. By describing three kinds of Judaic holy persons, I offer a set of three ideal types, which help us to sort out the diverse points of emphasis in that varied religious culture created by Jews living in the Land of Israel.

Third, we focus upon a single group, represented in the Gospels as one source of opposition to Jesus, namely, the Pharisees. I describe the problems we face in dealing with the Pharisees, who they were, and what they became.

Fourth, since New Testament students generally learn about the problems associated with the discovery of "the historical Jesus," I present a set of similar problems. The best-known figure in the

9

Judaism framed in the name of the Pharisees was Hillel. Some of the teachings attributed to him present parallels to teachings attributed to Jesus. Hillel, moreover, is generally supposed to have lived just about at the turn of the first Christian century. Accordingly, I provide a repertoire of sources about Hillel and some of the problems in interpreting those sources. The sources are not always readily accessible, but I provide what is needed to grasp their main points.

Finally, the catalytic event in the formation of the kind of Judaism we now know as normative—that is, the Judaism that took shape in the documents produced by rabbis from the first through the seventh centuries—was the destruction of the Temple in 70 C.E. That same event proved decisive in the formation of Christianity as an autonomous and self-conscious community of Israelite faith. So I conclude with a brief account of what later rabbis said about the meaning of the destruction, how it was understood and interpreted in the framework and context of Judaism.

These five chapters stand essentially independent of one another. Each is meant to serve as an individual reading. The first two may contribute to the beginning units of a New Testament course, those on the background in history and religion of Israel in the Land of Israel ("Judaism"). The next two may serve in the exposition of the parts of the Gospels that set Jesus into controversy with other Jews of his day, with emphasis, obviously, on the Pharisees. The final chapter may help to set nascent Christianity into the appropriate comparative setting with nascent Judaism. As indicated, chapter 4 may also prove useful in courses in which the critical historical issues in the study of "the Jesus of history" may find a measure of illumination in comparable, though not wholly parallel, problems in studying later narratives and traditions concerning historical rabbis of the same time and place.

Let me at the outset explain why formative Christianity demands to be studied in the context of formative Judaism, and formative Judaism in the context of formative Christianity. For throughout the history of the West, these two religious traditions, along with Islam, have struggled in competition with one another. While in numbers the competing parties were scarcely equal, in theological and moral power, each met its match in the other. What perpetually drew the one into competition with the other? Why could they not let one another be? These questions draw attention in our own setting, in modern times, after the Holocaust in particular, because, at last, the two great faiths of the West join together to confront a common challenge of renewal. So Judaism and Christianity work together in mutual respect, as never before, in the service of one humanity in the image of one God. We are able to ask these questions because the spirit of our own age permits us to discuss them irenically, in ways utterly without precedent in the centuries before our own so-tragic times.

Both Judaism and Christianity claim to be the heirs and products of the Hebrew Scriptures—*Tanakh* to the Jews, Old Testament to the Christians. Yet both great religious traditions derive not solely or directly from the authority and teachings of those Scriptures, but rather from the ways in which that authority has been mediated, and those teachings interpreted, through other holy books. The New Testament is the prism through which the light of the Old comes to Christianity. The canon of rabbinical writings is the star that guides Jews to the revelation of Sinai, the Torah. That canon consists of the Mishnah, a law code, ca. 200 C.E., the Talmud of the Land of Israel, ca. 400 C.E., a systematic exegesis of the Mishnah, the various collections of exegeses of Scriptures called *midrashim*, ca. 400–600 C.E., and the Talmud of Babylonia, also a systematic explanation of the Mishnah, ca. 500–600 C.E. All together, these writings constitute "the Oral Torah," that is, that body of tradition assigned to the authority of God's revelation to Moses at Mount Sinai. The claim of these two great Western religious traditions, in all their rich variety, is for the veracity not merely of Scriptures, but also of Scriptures as interpreted by the New Testament or the Babylonian Talmud (and associated rabbinical writings).

The Hebrew Scriptures produced the two interrelated, yet quite separate groups of religious societies that formed Judaism and Christianity. Developed along lines established during late antiquity, these societies in modern times come near to each other in the West. Here they live not merely side by side, but together. However, while most people are familiar with the story of the development of Christianity, few are fully aware that Judaism constitutes a separate and distinctive religious tradition. The differences are not limited to negations of Christian beliefs—"Jews do not believe in this or that"—but also extend to profound affirmations of Judaic ones. To understand the Judaic dissent, one must comprehend the Judaic affirmation in its own terms.

What is it that historical Judaism sought to build? What are its primary emphases, its evocative symbols? What lies at the heart of the human situation, as constructed and imagined by classical

Judaism? The answers come first of all from the pages of the rabbinic canon and related literature. From late antiquity onward, the rabbis of the Torah, written and oral, supplied the proof texts, constructed the society, shaped the values, occupied the mind, and formed the soul of Judaism. For all the human concerns brought by Christians to the figure of Christ, the Jews looked to Torah. Torah means revelation: first, the five books of Moses; later, the whole Hebrew Scriptures; still later, the Oral and Written Revelation of Sinai, embodied in the Mishnah and the Talmuds. Finally it comes to stand for, to symbolize, what in modern language is called "Judaism": the whole body of belief, doctrine, practice, patterns of piety and behavior, and moral and intellectual commitments that constitute the Judaic version of reality.

However, while the Christ-event stands at the beginning of the tradition of Christianity, the rabbinic canon comes at the end of the formation of the Judaism contained in it. It is the written record of the constitution of the life of Israel, the Jewish people, long after the principles and guidelines of that constitution had been worked out and effected in everyday life. Moreover, the early years of Christianity were dominated first by the figure of the Master, then his disciples and their followers bringing the gospel to the nations; the formative years of rabbinic Judaism saw a small group of men who were not dominated by a single leader but who effected an equally far-reaching revolution in the life of the Jewish nation.

Both the apostles and the rabbis thus reshaped the antecedent religion of Israel, and both claimed to be Israel. That pre-Christian, prerabbinic religion of Israel, for all its variety, exhibited common traits: belief in one God, reverence for and obedience to the revelation contained in the Hebrew Scriptures, veneration of the Temple in Jerusalem (while it stood), and expectation of the coming of a Messiah to restore all the Jews to Palestine and to bring to a close the anguish of history. The Christian Jews concentrated on the last point, proclaiming that the Messiah had come in Jesus; the rabbinic Jews focused on the second, teaching that only through the full realization of the imperatives of the Hebrew Scriptures, Torah, as interpreted and applied by the rabbis, would the people merit the coming of the Messiah. The rabbis, moreover, claimed alone to possess the whole Torah of Moses. This is central to their doctrine: Moses had revealed not only the message now written down in his books, but also an oral Torah, which was formulated and transmitted to his successors, and they to theirs, through Joshua, the prophets, the sages, scribes, and other holy men, and finally to the rabbis of the day. For the Christian, therefore, the issue of the Messiah predominated; for the rabbinic Jew, the issue of Torah; and for both, the question of salvation was crucial.

What form would Western civilization have taken had the Judaic, rather than the Christian, formulation of the heritage of Hebrew Scriptures come to predominate? What sort of society would have emerged? How would people have regulated their affairs? What would have been the shape of the prevailing value systems?

Behind the immense varieties of Christian life and Christian and post-Christian society stand the evocative teachings and theological and moral convictions assigned by Christian belief to the figure of Christ. To be a Christian in some measure meant, and means, to seek to be like him, in one of the many ways in which Christians envisaged him.

To be a Jew may similarly be reduced to the single, pervasive symbol of Judaism: Torah. To be a Jew meant to live the life of Torah, in one of the many ways in which the masters of Torah taught.

We know what the figure of Christ has meant to the art, music, and literature of the West; the church to its politics, history, and piety; Christian faith to its values and ideals. It is much harder to say what Torah would have meant to creative arts, the course of relations among nations and people, the hopes and aspirations of ordinary folk. For between Christ, universally known and triumphant, and Torah, the spiritual treasure of a tiny, harassed, abused people, seldom fully known and never long victorious, stands the abyss: mastery of the world on the one side, the sacrifice of the world on the other. Perhaps the difference comes at the very start when the Christians, despite horrendous suffering, determined to conquer and save the world and to create the new Israel. The rabbis, unmolested and unimpeded, set forth to transform and regenerate the old Israel. For the former, the arena of salvation was all humankind, the actor was a single man. For the latter, the course of salvation began with Israel, God's first love, and the stage was that singular but paradigmatic society, the Jewish people.

To save the world the apostle had to suffer in and for it, appear before magistrates, subvert empires. To redeem the Jewish people the rabbi had to enter into, share, and reshape the life of the community, deliberately eschew the politics of nations and patiently submit to empires. The vision of the apostle extended to all nations and peoples. Immediate suffering therefore was the welcome penalty to be paid for eventual, universal dominion. The rabbi's eye looked upon Israel, and, in his love for Jews, he sought not to achieve domination or to risk martyrdom, but rather to labor for social and spiritual transformation which was to be accomplished through the complete union of his life with that of the community. The one was prophet to the nations, the other, priest to the people. No wonder then that the apostle earned the crown of martyrdom, but prevailed in history; while the rabbi received martyrdom, when it came, only as one of and wholly within the people. He gave up the world and its conversion in favor of the people and their regeneration. In the end the people hoped that through their regeneration, if need be through their suffering, the world also would be redeemed. But the people would be the instrument, not the craftsmen, of redemption, which God alone would bring.

As a believing Jew, my prayer is that this modest book will help to bring peace in our time to our world.

J.N.

24 December 1982
8 Tebet 5743
The eve of the bar mitzvah of
my third son, Noam Mordechai Menahem.

ACKNOWLEDGMENTS

This book is a composite of parts of several previously published books of mine. Each has gone through several printings and editions. None was written in particular to meet the educational requirements of beginning students in New Testament studies. Self-evidently, none of them, read cover to cover, would serve very well in the setting of elementary courses in the New Testament and earliest Christianity. They intersect with, but are not devoted to, that subject. That is why I have chosen to present excerpts, each selected for a particular educational task.

In every instance I have made very substantial revisions. Chapter 2 has not been published previously at all.

I am grateful to my friend, Mr. Bernard Scharfstein, publisher of KTAV Publishing House, Inc., for permission to reprint the designated sections of three titles of mine under his imprint. I own all copyrights.

Preface
"Both Judaism and Christianity . . . ," to the end, in *There We Sat Down. Talmudic Judaism in the Making* (New York: KTAV Publishing House, 1978), 20–25.

Chapter 1
First Century Judaism in Crisis: Yohanan ben Zakkai and the Renaissance of Torah (New York: KTAV Publishing House, 1982), 21–43.

Chapter 3
From Politics to Piety: The Emergence of Pharisaic Judaism (New York: KTAV Publishing House, 1979), 1–11, 143–54.

Chapter 4
From Politics to Piety, 13–44.

Chapter 5
First Century Judaism in Crisis, 156–75.

ACKNOWLEDGMENTS

I earnestly request colleagues who use this book to tell me how I can revise it, in a future edition, to make it more useful to their teaching about the world, in Judaism, in which Christianity came into being. I should look forward to both revising the chapters in this book and adding new chapters to cover topics important to the beginning student but neglected here. In that way I may make a contribution to better understanding between the two great religious traditions of the West.

I owe special thanks to my teacher and friend, Professor W. D. Davies, now at Texas Christian University, Fort Worth, for detailed criticisms of the manuscript, most of which I was able to accommodate. I also appreciate the helpful comments and criticism of my dear friends Professors Etienne Trocmé, University of Strasbourg, Martin Hengel, University of Tübingen, and Birger Gerhardsson, University of Lund. It is especially pleasing to note that while Professor Gerhardsson and I differ on some matters of fact and interpretation, he nonetheless has taken a keen interest in my work and given his time and learning to help improve it.

It has been a real pleasure to work on a book with Mr. Norman Hjelm and his colleagues at Fortress Press. While I cannot point to a single unhappy experience with editors and publishers in a quarter century of publishing books, I still have to regard the encounter with Fortress as especially pleasant.

The dedication of this book is to a young colleague, formerly a graduate student at Brown University, whose friendship, wise counsel, unflagging good sense, and loyalty sustained me in a very difficult year in my life. I believe that Robert Berchman will become one of the scholarly ornaments of his generation. He already is a source of both joy and also steady, sane advice for all his friends. This is my token of thanks and recognition for devotion beyond the call of duty.

J. N.

1
THE WORLD
OF
JESUS' PEOPLE

JERUSALEM AND THE TEMPLE

From near and far pilgrims climbed the paths to Jerusalem. Distant lands sent their annual tribute, taxes imposed by a spiritual rather than a worldly sovereignty. Everywhere Jews turned to the Temple mountain when they prayed. Although Jews differed about matters of law and theology, the meaning of history, and the timing of the Messiah's arrival, most affirmed the holiness of the city Isaiah called Ariel, Jerusalem, the faithful city. It was here that the sacred drama of the day must be enacted. And looking backward, we know they were right. It was indeed the fate of Jerusalem which in the end shaped the faith of Judaism for endless generations to come—but not quite in the ways that most people expected before 70 C.E.

How had Jerusalem cast its spell upon the Jews of far-off lands, to bring them together in their hearts' yearning? For centuries Israel had sung with the psalmist, "Our feet were standing within thy courts, O Jerusalem." They had exulted, "Pray for the peace of Jerusalem! May all prosper who seek your welfare!" Jews long contemplated the lessons of the old destruction. They were sure that by learning what Jeremiah, Ezekiel, and (Second) Isaiah taught about the meaning of the catastrophe of 586 B.C.E., by keeping the faith that prophecy demanded, they had ensured the city's eternity. Even then the Jews were a very old people. Their own records, translated into the language of all civilized people, testified to their antiquity. They could look back upon ancient enemies now forgotten by history, and ancient disasters, the spiritual lessons of which illumined current times. People thought that they kept the faith by devotion to the holy city, to the sacred Temple, to divinely ordained rites of service, to the priesthood, to the altar. And many a Jew yearned to see the priests upon their platform, to hear the Levites in their great choir singing the songs of David, to receive the blessing of the Lord in the Temple in Jerusalem. If people thought they kept the faith, they had good reason. What had the Lord commanded of old, which now they did not do? For three sins the ancient temple had fallen in 586 B.C.E.— murder, adultery, and idolatry. Now, five centuries later, idolatry was a grotesque memory. Murder and adultery were surely not so common among those whom God had instructed as elsewhere, they supposed. As to ancient Scriptures, were these not studied in the synagogues Sabbath upon Sabbath? But the most certain testimony of all to the enduring covenant was the Temple, which stood as the nexus between Jew and God. Its services bore witness to Israel's enduring loyalty to the covenant and the commandments of Sinai. They saw Jerusalem with the eye of faith, and that vision transformed the city.

The activity was endless. Priests hurried to and fro, important because of their tribe, sacred because of their task, officiating at the sacrifices morning and eventide, busying themselves through the day with the Temple's needs. They were always careful to keep the levitical rules of purity which God decreed, they thought, for just this place and hour. Levites assisting them and responsible for the public liturgies could be seen everywhere. In the outer courts Jews from all parts of the world, speaking many languages, changed their foreign money for the Temple coin. They brought up their *sheqel,* together with the free will, or peace, or sin, or other offerings they were liable to give. Outside, in the city beyond, artisans created the necessary vessels or repaired broken ones. Incense makers mixed spices. Animal dealers selected the most perfect beasts. In the schools young priests were taught the ancient law, to which in time they would conform as had their ancestors before them, exactly as did their fathers that very day. All the population either directly or indirectly was engaged in some way in the work of the Temple. The city lived for it, by it, and on its revenues. In modern terms, Jerusalem was a center of pilgrimage, and its economy was based upon tourism.

But no one saw things in such a light. Jerusalem had an industry, to be sure, but if a Jew were asked, "What is the business of this city?" he would have replied without guile, "It is a holy city, and its work is the service of God on high." Only a few people doubted it. For reasons of their own, those who formed the commune at the Dead Sea abandoned the Temple, regarding it as hopelessly impure, its calendar as erroneous. Others, the Pharisees, thought that the priests should conduct themselves in accordance with the oral tradition they believed God had revealed to Moses at Sinai, that Moses had transmitted to the prophets, and the prophets to sages, down to that very day and to their own group. But even they were among the Temple's loyal servants. The Temple was the center of the world. They said the mount was the highest hill in the world. To it in time would come the anointed of God. In the meantime, they taught, the Temple sacrifice was the way to serve God, a way he himself in remotest times had decreed. True, there were other ways believed to be more important, for the prophets had emphasized that sacrifice alone was not enough to reconcile the sinner to a God made angry by unethical or immoral behavior. Morality, ethics, humility, good faith—these, too, he required. But good faith meant loyalty to the covenant which had specified, among other things, that the priests do just what they were doing. The animal sacrifices, the incense, the oil, wine, and bread were to be arrayed in the service of the Most High.

"BECAUSE OF THEIR SINS"

Later, people condemned this generation of the first Christian century. Christians and Jews alike reflected upon the destruction of the great sanctuary. They looked to the alleged misdeeds of those who lived at the time for reasons to account for the destruction. No generation in the history of Jewry had been so roundly, universally condemned by posterity as that of Yohanan ben Zakkai. Christians remembered, in the tradition of the church, that Jesus wept over the city and said a bitter, sorrowing sentence:

> O Jerusalem, Jerusalem, killing the prophets and stoning those who are sent to you! How often would I have gathered your children together as a hen gathers her brood under her wings, and you would not! Behold, your house is forsaken and desolate. For I tell you, you will not see me again, until you say, "Blessed is he who comes in the name of the Lord" (Matt. 23:37–39).

And when the disciples pointed out the Temple buildings from a distance, he said to them, "You see all these, do you not? Truly, I say to you, there will not be left here one stone upon another, that will not be thrown down" (Matt. 24:2; cf. Luke 21:6.). So for twenty centuries, Jerusalem was seen through the eye of Christian faith as a faithless city, killing prophets, and therefore desolated by the righteous act of a wrathful God.

But Jews said no less. From the time of the destruction, they prayed: "On account of our sins we have been exiled from our land,

and we have been removed far from our country. We cannot go up to appear and bow down before you, to carry out our duties in your chosen Sanctuary, in the great and holy house upon which your name was called." It is not a great step from "our sins" to "the sins of the generation in whose time the Temple was destroyed." It is not a difficult conclusion, and not a few have reached it. The Temple was destroyed mainly because of the sins of the Jews of that time, particularly "causeless hatred." Whether the sins were those specified by Christians or by talmudic rabbis hardly matters. This was supposed to be a sinning generation.

It was *not* a sinning generation, but one deeply faithful to the covenant and to the Scripture that set forth its terms, perhaps more so than many who have since condemned it. First-century Israelites sinned only by their failure. Had they overcome Rome, even in the circles of the rabbis they would have found high praise, for success indicates the will of Providence. But on what grounds are they to be judged sinners? The Temple was destroyed, but it was destroyed because of a brave and courageous, if hopeless, war. That war was waged not for the glory of a king or for the aggrandizement of a people, but in the hope that at its successful conclusion, pagan rule would be extirpated from the holy land. This was the articulated motive. It was a war fought explicitly for the sake and in the name of God. The struggle called forth prophets and holy men, leaders whom the people did not kill or stone, but courageously followed past all hope of success. Jews were not demoralized or cowardly, afraid to die because they had no faith in what they were doing, fearful to dare because they did not want to take risks. The Jerusalemites fought with amazing courage, despite unbelievable odds. Since they lost, later generations looked for their sin, for none could believe that the omnipotent God would permit his Temple to be destroyed for no reason. As after 586 B.C.E., so after 70 C.E., the alternative was this: "Either our fathers greatly sinned, or God is not just." The choice thus represented no choice at all. "God is just, but we have sinned— we, but mostly our fathers before us. Therefore, all that has come upon us—the famine, the exile, the slavery to pagans—these are just recompense for our own deeds."

HEROD AND ROMAN RULE

The Jews were ruled, just before the turn of the first century, by King Herod, a Roman ally and a strong and able monarch. Herod's sons took over after his death, just before the turn of the century.

What was Herod's position within the larger Roman context, and why did he, as a native Jew, enjoy Roman support and allegiance? It was imperial policy in Herod's time to exert authority through territorial monarchs, petty kings who ruled frontier territories still too unruly to receive a Roman viceroy. Rome later came to govern the protectorates through its own agents. It finally incorporated the subjugated lands into the normal provincial structure. Thus in Armenia, Cilicia, and other territories on the Parthian frontier Rome established or supported friendly kings, ethnarchs, and tetrarchs, thereby governing through subservient agents in lands where Rome itself did not choose to rule. Honored by Rome with the titles *Socius et Amicus Populi Romani,* "associate and friend of Roman people," and, in the East, *Philo-Romaios* and *Philo-Kaiser,* "friend of Rome," "friend of Caesar," Herod governed efficiently. He collected revenues, contrived public works to develop vast tracts of land and eliminate unemployment, and, as we have seen, constructed a magnificent temple in Jerusalem. He also built several large cities, fortresses, and palaces including Herodion in the south, Sebaste in Samaria, and Caesarea, a seaport in the Sharon. Herod stabilized political life, which had been in turmoil during the reign of the last Hasmonean monarchs. Indeed, under him there were no politics at all, only palace intrigue and slaughter of potentially dangerous wives, sons, and servants. Most Jews simply could not participate in public affairs. Many retired from the stage of political history. Earlier institutions of political life were either transformed into instruments of state, like the high priesthood, or apparently ignored, like the Sanhedrin. Under Herod, official culture came more and more under Hellenistic domination. Court history was written in Greek by able Syrians such as Nicholaus of Damascus. The Temple cult was managed by agents of the monarchy, men who purchased the high priesthood at a price, held it at the king's pleasure, and, enriched by the priestly dues, handed it in the accepted Greek manner to the next appointee. It was a brilliant reign, but in the wrong time and over the wrong people.

After Herod's death in 6 B.C.E., the people begged for direct Roman government. "They implored the Romans to unite their country to Syria and to entrust its administration to Roman governors. The Jews would then show that, though people said they were factious and always at war, they knew how to obey equitable rulers." The Romans tried to keep Herod's sons in power, but when this led to further difficulties, they acquiesced and appointed the first in a line of procurators. The procurators did not share Herod's interest in developing the economy by building port cities and roads. They were mainly concerned with the imperial welfare, if not, first of all, with their own. They lived in Hellenistic Caesarea, went up to Jerusalem when masses of pilgrims came up to celebrate the festivals, and were glad to return to the cosmopolitan capital as soon as possible. When, in the spring of 66 c.e., one of them, Cestius, did not survive a bloody ambush on the road back, the revolution began. The procuratorial government ended as abruptly as it had begun.

ECONOMIC LIFE

The first act of procuratorial government was normally to divide the conquered territory into municipal districts; the second was to take a census, determining the rate at which cities could be expected to contribute to the treasury. Taxes were applied to men, houses, animals, sales, imports, and exports (at a moderate rate) and were collected by an efficient bureaucracy. Besides these taxes, Jews paid dues to another sovereignty as well, that imposed by the ancestral faith. The Bible had detailed many kinds of priestly and levitical offerings and animal sacrifices to support the expensive Temple cult. Under a priestly government these taxes would certainly have supported a large administration. This doubtless was the economic rationale for the multitudinous tithes and offerings. Although the priests had ceased to rule, they still claimed their dues. With Roman help they obtained some of them from the majority of Jews and all from the very pious. Throughout these years Jews thus were paying a twofold tax. The extent of civil and religious taxation has been estimated at from thirty to forty percent of the gross national income, but it was probably considerably lower since the majority of the Jews paid only a small part of the religious imposts.

In any event the Jews never regarded Roman rule as legitimate. Taxes were therefore seen to be robbery. The Pharisaic sages made no distinction between a tax collector and a thief or an extortioner. Sages regarded gentile rulers in Palestine as robbers, without any rights whatsoever either in the land or over its inhabitants. No pagan power whatever had any right in the land. No land acquisition could free a field user from the obligation to pay the tithes. Even if a gentile bought land from a Jew, he was held to be a sharecropper. No gentile could ever take valid, legal possession of any part of the land. This attitude to the rightful ownership of the land affected collection of taxes and much else, as we shall see. But religious imposts were something else again. The Pharisees believed they must be paid. Pharisees therefore separated themselves from Jews who neglected the tithes and heave-offerings or paid only part of them. It was one of the main distinctions between the Pharisaic masters and disciples, on the one hand, and the common people on the other. The former were meticulous in paying the priestly and levitical dues, and the latter were not.

Roman rule was advantageous for some. It opened the way for the adventurous to undertake vast enterprises in commerce and travel. Many took advantage of the opportunities of the Roman Empire to move to more prosperous lands. Throughout this period one discovers Jews settling in the most remote corners of the empire and beyond. Those who stayed at home benefited from economic stability.

Situated on the trade routes to the east and south, the coastal cities, which contained large Jewish minority populations, imported new wares for sale in the bazaars and markets of back country towns like Jerusalem. The Jewish economy in the land flourished. Roman peace, Herodian enterprise, the natural endowments of the land, and broad economic opportunities combined to yield an adequate subsistence in a relatively stable economy for a very large population.

Living standards nonetheless were modest. Archaeologists have not turned up pretentious synagogues, treasures of gems, rich pottery, furnishings, or costly sarcophagi dating from the first century. Life was simple. People ate cheap foods such as salted fish, bread made from low grades of local wheat, low quality grain imported from Egypt, or barley. They drank beer or wine diluted with water and sweetened their food with honey. Meat was eaten mostly on festival occasions, fish on the Sabbath. Judea was famed for its date palms, and the palm tree was sometimes engraved on coins as the emblem of the land. Most lived by farming or handicrafts. Contemporary parables borrow the imagery of fishing, agriculture, and petty trade. Few related to large-scale commerce, since Jews were mainly farmers and craftsmen. Riches meant a long-term food supply or a good wife. No parables refer to sophisticated problems of government, but many allude to a majestic, exalted monarch much magnified from the viewpoint of the mute populace.

EDUCATION

Many of the people, rich and poor alike, received an education in the main disciplines of Jewish tradition. This education, centering on religious learning, was sufficiently broad to impart civilizing and humanizing lessons. What did ordinary people study? They learned the Holy Scriptures. They, therefore, considered the history of the world from creation onward. They were taught in lessons about their forefathers, Abraham, Isaac, and Jacob, to emulate patriarchal hospitality to others and faithfulness to God. They studied about the life and laws of Moses. From those laws they gained an idea of how a covenanted community should conduct its affairs. They were instructed about their obligations to the poor, weak, orphaned, homeless, the stranger, and the outsider. They were educated to say that God is one, and that there are no other gods. They were told about the prophets whom God had sent to warn before ancient disasters and to exhort afterward. Those prophets had said that what God wanted of people was that they do justice, love mercy, and walk humbly before God. The people learned that Providence guided their fate and that nothing happened but that God decreed it. So they were taught to look for the meaning of daily and cosmic events alike. A comet, drought, broken leg, or earthquake—all could equally convey a truth. In the biblical writings they studied the wisdom of ancient sages, learning prudence, piety, and understanding.

In modern terms their curriculum included much attention to matters of metaphysics, law and morality, ethics and history. Such lessons were intended to create a decent human being. Perhaps everyday conduct revealed something of their impact but it was the historical lesson that seems to have had the greatest effect. God had given the land to Israel. Pagans had held it for a time, because in ancient days the people had sinned. But Israel had gotten it back after God had purified the people through suffering. In time, God again would set things straight and send a king like David of old, anointed in the manner of the ancient monarchy, to sit upon Mount Zion and dispense justice and revelation to all nations.

SOCIAL CLASSES

Class divisions were complicated by the regional variations of the land. Jerusalem was the metropolis of the Jews. Its populace included a significant number of wealthy people, both absentee landlords and great merchants, as well as many priests who lived on the priestly dues and Temple endowments. The city also contained a smaller class of Levites, who performed certain nonsacrificial tasks in the sanctuary and managed the buildings. Artisans whose skills were indispensable in the building and maintenance of the Temple, petty traders, a large urban proletariat, and unskilled laborers filled the crowded streets. Jerusalemites tended to separate themselves from the Judean provincials for both social and ritual reasons. Living in close proximity to the sanctuary, the inhabitants of the city were more concerned about observing the requirements of ritual cleanness, imposed by residence in the holy place, than were the provincials who purified themselves mainly for the festal pilgrimages. The provincials often did not have the benefit of much advanced education. Animosities between urban and rural residents were bitter. The provincials themselves were by no means united. The country gentry, landowners holding considerable property in the fertile lowland plains, had less in common with their highland neighbors than with the urban upper bourgeoisie.

On the other hand, the rural farmers and proletarian submerged classes were divorced from the main issues of national life. They welcomed the ministry of powerful personalities, sometimes sages empowered by learning, but more often wonderworkers able to heal mind and body. Jericho and the Southern Plain were the main centers of the rural gentry. On the rocky Judean hills lived the rural yeomanry and proletariat. In Galilee class divisions between wealthier and poorer peasants likewise were manifest. Hundreds of rural villages, large and small, clustered in the fertile hills and valleys of the north. Only Sepphoris and Tiberias were large urban centers, and they did not dominate the province as Jerusalem did Judea.

THE SECTS:
ESSENES, SADDUCEES, PHARISEES

The main social and religious events of this period held little interest for contemporary historians. Josephus, for one, paid very little attention to the inner life of Israel in his rich narrative of politics and war. His histories provide evidence that the masses had turned away from public affairs. They may have responded to changes in their political situation. They may have felt growing impatience with social inequity or with the alien government whose benefits were not obvious to them. Only in the riots and continuous unrest toward the end of this period, however, does their response become entirely evident. A few indicated their disapproval of the course of events by withdrawing from the common society. Some became hermits; some fled to other lands or entered monastic communities in which contact with the outside world was minimal.

The monastic commune near the shores of the Dead Sea was one such group. To the barren heights came people seeking purity and hoping for eternity. The purity they sought was not from common dirt, but from the uncleanness of this world, symbolized by contact with the impure insects or objects Scripture had declared unclean. In their

25

minds that uncleanness carried a far deeper meaning. This age was impure and therefore would soon be coming to an end. Those who wanted to do the Lord's service should prepare themselves for a holy war at the end of time. The commune at the Dead Sea, therefore, divided by ranks under captains, lived under military discipline and studied the well-known holy books as well as books others did not know about. These books specified when and how the holy war would be fought and the manner of life of those worthy to fight it. Men and women came to Qumran with their property, which they contributed to the common fund. There they prepared for a fateful day, not too long to be postponed, scarcely looking backward at those remaining in the corruption of this world. These Jews would be the last, smallest, "saving remnant" of all. Yet through them all humankind would come to know the truth. They prepared for Armageddon, and their battle against forces of ritual impurity, evil, and sin alike was for the Lord. The Qumran commune ordained: "This is the regulation for the men of the commune, who devote themselves to turn away from all evil, and to hold fast to all that he has commanded as his will, to separate themselves from the congregation of men of iniquity to be a commune in Torah and property." Likewise the psalmist of Qumran prayed:

Only as you draw a man near will I love him.
And as you keep him far away, so will I abominate him.

The members of wilderness communes described by Philo as Essenes avoided the settled society of town and city "because of the inequities which have become inveterate among city dwellers, for they know that their company would have a deadly effect upon their own souls." The communards sanctified themselves by meticulous observance of the rules of ritual purity and tried to found such a society as they thought worthy of receiving God's approval. Strikingly, they held that God himself had revealed to Moses the very laws they now obeyed.

Pharisees, probably meaning Separatists, of whom we hear more in chapters 3 and 4, also believed that all was not in order with the world. But they chose another way, likewise attributed to mosaic legislation. They remained within the common society in accordance with the teaching of Hillel, "Do not separate yourself from the community." The Pharisaic community therefore sought to rebuild society on its own ruins with its own mortar and brick. They differed among themselves. Some, called Zealots, accepted the Pharisaic interpretation of tradition, but thought to restore the fortune of

Israel through war. Others focused their efforts in the spiritual reform of the nation. The Pharisees actively fostered their opinions on tradition and religion among the whole people. According to Josephus, "They are able greatly to influence the masses of people. Whatever the people do about divine worship, prayers, and sacrifices, they perform according to their direction. The cities give great praise to them on account of their virtuous conduct, both in the actions of their lives and their teachings also." Though Josephus exaggerated the extent of their power, the Pharisees certainly exerted some influence in the religious life of Israel before they finally came to power in 70 C.E.

Among those sympathetic to the Pharisaic cause were some who entered into an urban religious communion, a mostly unorganized society known as the fellowship (*havurah*). The basis of this society was meticulous observance of laws of tithing and other priestly offerings as well as the rules of ritual purity outside the Temple where they were not mandatory. The members undertook to eat even profane foods (not sacred tithes or other offerings) in a state of rigorous levitical cleanness. At table, they compared themselves to Temple priests at the altar. These rules tended to segregate the members of the fellowship, for they ate only with those who kept the law as they thought proper. The fellows thus mediated between the obligation to observe religious precepts and the injunction to remain within the common society. By keeping the rules of purity the fellow separated from the common man, but by remaining within the towns and cities of the land, he preserved the possibility of teaching others by example. The fellows lived among, but not with, the people of the land. With neither formal structure nor officers and bylaws as at Qumran, the fellowship represented the polity of people who recognized one another as part of the same inchoate community. They formed a new, if limited, society within the old. They were the few who kept what they held to be the faith in the company of the many who did not.

Upper-class opinion was expressed in the viewpoint of still another group, the Sadducees. They stood for strict adherence to the written word in religious matters, conservatism in both ritual and belief. Their name probably derived from the priesthood of Zaddoq, established by David ten centuries earlier. They differed from the Pharisees especially on the doctrine of revelation. They acknowledged Scripture as the only authority, themselves as its sole arbiters. They denied that its meaning might be elucidated by the Pharisees' allegedly ancient traditions attributed to Moses or by the Pharisaic devices of exegesis and scholarship. The Pharisees claimed that Scripture and the traditional oral interpretation were one. To the Sadducees such a claim of unity was spurious and masked innovation. They differed also on the eternity of the soul. The Pharisees believed in the survival of the soul, the revival of the body, the day of judgment, and life in the world to come. The Sadducees found nothing in Scripture that to their way of thinking supported such doctrines. They ridiculed both these ideas and the exegesis that made them possible. They won over the main body of officiating priests and wealthier men. With the destruction of the Temple their ranks were decimated. Very little literature later remained to preserve their viewpoint. It is difficult indeed to compare them to the other sects. They may have constituted no social institution like the Pharisaic and Essenic groups. In their day, however, the Sadducees claimed to be the legitimate heirs of Israel's faith. Holding positions of power and authority, they succeeded in leaving so deep an impression on society that even their Pharisaic, Essenic, and Christian opponents did not wholly wipe out their memory.

The Sadducees were most influential among landholders and merchants, the Pharisees among the middle and lower urban classes, the Essenes among the disenchanted of both these classes. These classes and sectarian divisions manifested a vigorous inner life, with politics revolving about peculiarly Jewish issues such as matters of exegesis, law, doctrine, and the meaning of history. The vitality of Israel would have astonished the Roman administration, and when it burst forth, it did.

CONVERSION: "NORMATIVE JUDAISM"?

The rich variety of Jewish religious expression in this period ought not to obscure the fact that for much of Jewish Palestine, Judaism was a relatively new phenomenon. Herod was the grandson of pagans. Similarly, the entire Galilee had been converted to Judaism only one hundred and twenty years before the Common Era. In the later expansion of the Hasmonean kingdom, other regions were forcibly brought within the fold. The Hasmoneans used Judaism imperially, as a means of winning the loyalty of the pagan Semites in the regions of Palestine they conquered. But in a brief period of three or four generations the deeply rooted practices of the Semitic natives of Galilee, Idumea, and other areas could not have been wiped out. They were rather covered over with a veneer of monotheism. Hence the newly converted territories, though vigorously loyal to their new faith, were no more Judaized in so short a time than were the later Russians, Poles, Celts, or Saxons Christianized within a century.

It took a great effort to transform an act of circumcision of the flesh, joined with a mere verbal affirmation of one God, done under severe duress, into a deepening commitment to faith. And yet in the war of 66 C.E. the Jews of newly converted regions fought with great loyalty. While the Galileans had proved unable to stand upon the open battlefield, many of them together with Idumeans retreated to the holy city. There they gave their lives in the last great cataclysms of the war. The exceptional loyalty of the newly converted regions would lead one to suppose that it was to the Temple cult, to the God whom it served, and to the nation that supported it that the pagan Semites were originally converted. They could have known little of the more difficult service of the heart through study of Torah and ethical and moral action which the Pharisees demanded.

While the central teachings of the faith were very ancient, adherence of many who professed it was therefore only relatively recent and superficial. The Pharisaic party, dating at least from the second century B.C.E., if not much earlier, never solidly established itself in Galilee before the second century C.E. The religious beliefs of recently converted people could not have encompassed ideas and issues requiring substantial study, elaborate schooling, and a well-established pattern of living. Conversion of one group to another faith never obliterates the former culture, but rather entails the translation of the new into the idiom of the old, so that in the end it results in a modification of both. The newly Judaized regions similarly must have preserved substantial remnants of their former pagan Semitic and Hellenistic cultures. The inhabitants could not have been greatly changed merely by receiving "Judaism," which meant in the beginning little more than submitting to the knife of the circumcizer rather than to the sword of the slaughterer. Only after many generations was the full implication of conversion realized in the lives of the people in Galilee, and then mainly because great centers of tannaitic law and teaching were established among them.

For this period, however, no such thing as "normative Judaism" existed, from which one or another "heretical" group might diverge. Not only in the great center of the faith, Jerusalem, do we find numerous competing groups, but throughout the country and abroad we may discern a religious tradition in the midst of great flux. It was full of vitality, but in the end without a clear and widely accepted view of what was required of each individual, apart from acceptance of mosaic revelation. And this could mean whatever you wanted. People would ask one teacher after another, "What must I do to enter the kingdom of heaven?" precisely because no authoritative answer existed. In the end two groups emerged, the Christians and the rabbis, heirs of the Pharisaic sages. Each offered an all-encompassing interpretation of Scripture, explaining what it did and did not mean. Each promised salvation for individuals and for Israel as a whole. Of the two, the rabbis achieved somewhat greater success among the Jews. Wherever the rabbis' views of Scripture were propagated the Christian view of the meaning of biblical, especially prophetic, revelation and its fulfillment made relatively little progress. This was true, specifically, in Jewish Palestine itself, in certain cities in Mesopotamia, and in central Babylonia. Where the rabbis were not to be found, as in Egyptian Alexandria, Syria, Asia Minor, Greece, and in the West, Christian biblical interpretation and salvation through Christ risen from the dead found a ready audience among the Jews. It was not without good reason that the gospel tradition of Matthew saw in the "scribes and Pharisees" the chief opponents of Jesus' ministry. Whatever the historical facts of that ministry, the rabbis proved afterward to be the greatest stumbling block for the Christian mission to the Jews.

SELF-GOVERNMENT

It was a peculiar circumstance of Roman imperial policy that facilitated the growth of such a vigorous inner life and permitted the development of nonpolitical institutions to express it. Rome carefully respected Jewish rights to limited self-government. The populace was subject to its own law and quarrels were adjudicated by its own judges. Rome had specific and clearly defined purposes for the empire. Her policies could be adequately effected without totalitarian interference in the inner affairs of the conquered peoples. The same indifference to local sensitivities that very occasionally permitted a procurator to bring his military standards into a city pure of "graven images" likewise encouraged him to ignore territorial affairs of considerable weight.

The national tribunal, called variously the Sanhedrin or High Court, acted with a measure of freedom to determine internal policy in religion, ritual, cult, and local law. The Sanhedrin lost authority to inflict capital punishment, it is generally assumed, shortly after Judea became a part of the Syrian provincial administration. Whether, in fact, it had administered the death penalty in Herod's reign is not entirely clear. The court certainly maintained the right to direct Temple affairs. It decided matters of civil and commercial law and torts and defined personal and family status and marriage procedure. The court also collected the biblical levies and determined the sacred calendar. It thus represented the one abiding institutional expression of Israel's inner autonomy during the procuratorial regime. Both the Pharisees and Sadducees took an active interest in the religious, social, and economic administration of Israel's life. The Sanhedrin provided a means to formulate and effect these interests. The leaders of both major viewpoints played a considerable part in the nation's autonomous affairs. The exact nature of Jewish self-government and the institutions that embodied it has not yet been finally clarified. The sources are difficult; no body of sources presents a picture that can be wholly verified in some other independent tradition. It seems to me the most likely view for the present is that of Professor E. E. Urbach:

> There was one Sanhedrin, the one that met in the Hewn Chamber. . . . The Sanhedrin adjoined the altar. . . . It was a court composed of priests, Levites and Israelites who may give their daughters in marriage to priests. . . . The High Priest was permitted to preside at the Sanhedrin. . . . Throughout its existence the institution was enveloped by an aura of sanctity and supreme authority, and just as the holiness of the Temple was not impaired in the estimation of the Sages by the High Priests who were unworthy of officiating, so it never entered their minds to repudiate the institution of the Sanhedrin or to set up a rival to it in the form of a competing court. They endeavored rather to exercise their influence and to introduce their rulings and views even into the ritual of the Temple service and into the Sanhedrin's methods of operation. They did not always enjoy success, and not infrequently clashed with High Priests as well as with other bureaucrats and officeholders.

WOMEN

While women play a prominent part in the Gospels' lives of Jesus, they constituted a subordinated caste. In important ways they took second place. First of all, the Temple cult, so critical in the nation's understanding of the world, lay entirely in the hands of men. Women could not enter the innermost parts of the Temple or actually share in the cult by serving as priests. Accordingly, when it came to the processes of sanctification carried on in the Temple, women stood along the sides but never at the center; the women's court was set away from the holy altar itself, and that fact captured the position of women in society as a whole. Yet Scripture, for its part, knew women in numerous roles of leadership and influence, beginning with Miriam, sister of Moses, extending through prophets and savior figures, for example, Huldah, in the time of Jeremiah, and Esther, later on. Women played a central role in the political life of the country, both in ancient Israel and also in the century before the coming of Jesus, as well as at points in between.

Accordingly, in politics and in religion, women found for themselves important places everywhere but in the Temple itself. Yet, it surely is a fact that God was imagined, in general, as male, not female, and man, not woman, dominated. In the later laws of the Mishnah, preserving both rules and attitudes of the period at hand, woman is regarded as anomalous, man the norm and normal. In all, therefore, the position of women in first-century Israelite society exhibited those contradictory trends we find earlier and later. Where the priestly tradition dominated, there women were excluded. Perhaps, to begin with, the ancient pagan traditions of women as cult prostitutes led the framers of the Israelite priestly code to keep women out of the cult and Temple altogether. Whatever the original motive, the result, for centuries to come, proved disastrous.

CONCLUSION

Jesus came into a world of irrepressible conflict. That conflict was between two pieties, two universal conceptions of what the world required. On the one hand, the Roman imperialist thought that good government, that is, Roman government, must serve to keep the peace. Rome would bring the blessings of civil order and material progress to many lands. For the Roman that particular stretch of hills, farmland, and desert that Jews called "the Land of Israel" meant little economically, but a great deal strategically. No wealth could be hoped for, but to lose Palestine would mean to lose the keystone of empire in the East. We see Palestine from the perspective of the West. It appears as a land bridge between Egypt and Asia Minor, the corner of a major trade route. But to the imperial strategist, Palestine loomed as the bulwark of the eastern frontier against Parthia. The Parthians, holding the Tigris-Euphrates frontier, were a mere few hundred miles from Palestine, separated by a desert no one could control. If the Parthians could take Palestine, Egypt would fall into their hands. Parthian armies moreover were pointed like a sword toward Antioch and the seat of empire established there. Less than a century earlier they had actually captured Jerusalem and seated upon its throne a puppet of their own. For a time they thrust Roman rule out of the eastern shores of the Mediterranean.

For Rome, therefore, Palestine was too close to the most dangerous frontier of all to be given up. Indeed, among all the Roman frontiers only the oriental one was now contested by a civilized and dangerous foe. Palestine lay behind the very lines upon which that enemy had to be met. Rome could ill afford such a loss. Egypt, moreover, was her granary, the foundation of her social welfare and wealth. The grain of Egypt sustained the masses of Rome herself. Economic and military considerations thus absolutely required the retention of Palestine. Had Palestine stood in a less strategic locale, matters might have been different. Rome had a second such frontier territory to consider—Armenia. While she fought vigorously to retain predominance over the northern gateway to the Middle East, she generally remained willing to compromise on joint suzerainty with Parthia in Armenia—but not in Palestine.

For the Jews, the Land of Israel meant something of even greater import. They believed that history depended upon what happened in the Land of Israel. They thought that from creation to end of time the events that took place in Jerusalem would shape the fate of all humankind. Theirs, no less than Rome's, was an imperial view of the world, but with this difference: the empire was God's. If Rome could not lose Palestine, the Jew was unwilling to give up the Land of Israel. Rome scrupulously would do everything possible to please Jewry, permitting the Jews to keep their laws in exchange only for peaceful acquiescence to Roman rule. There was, alas, nothing Rome could actually do to please Jewry but evacuate Palestine. No amiable tolerance of local custom could suffice to win the people's submission.

Three Types
of Judaism in
the Age of Jesus

2
SAGE, PRIEST, MESSIAH

IDEAL TYPES

The holy men of Judaism divide into a number of distinct types; each figure with his point of stress and insistence, the thing that made him holy. (We speak of men only. In the period under discussion, women did not take a public and prominent part in Judaism.) Each kind of holy man represented a particular focus within the diverse religious tradition of Judaism. The three were: first, the priest; second, the sage or scribe or wise man; and third, the Messiah. Each stood for a different sort of holy way of life, pointed toward a different aspect of what God wanted from, or promised for, Israel, the Jewish people.

The scribe or sage (later "rabbi") centered on the Torah, the revelation of God to Moses at Mount Sinai, and laid stress upon study and interpretation and application of the teachings of the Torah to the everyday life of the Jewish people.

The priest centered on the Temple. He believed in serving God through sacrifice. He stressed the issue of holiness or sanctification.

People who looked forward to the near-at-hand coming of the Messiah emphasized the issue of salvation. They thought that great public events bore deep meaning for Israel's life, and so gave great emphasis to preparing now for an end that was coming soon.

While, we all know, Jesus was represented as Christ, the Messiah, New Testament writers also treat him as the perfect priest and sacrifice, as in the Epistle to the Hebrews. They further represent him as a great sage, teacher, hence "rabbi," as in the Gospels. Accordingly, in the figure of Jesus, the principal motifs of Judaism were drawn together. Later on, in the aftermath of the destruction of the Temple, the same points of emphasis would coalesce in the kind of Judaism that emerged from ancient times, represented, as we saw earlier, in the canon of the rabbinic writings, the Mishnah, the two Talmuds, and related books.

In positing three ideal types of Israelite piety—priest, scribe, Messiah—we must suspend for the moment our disbelief that things can have ever been so simple. We recognize the opposite. The troops of a messianic army led by Bar Kokba, 132–135 C.E., also observed Scripture's sacred calendar. Their goal was not only to enthrone the King-Messiah, their general, but also to rebuild the Temple, reestablish the priesthood, and restore the sacrificial cult. The Essene community at Qumran joined together the themes and streams we for the moment treat as separate: priesthood, Messiah, Torah-study. Among earliest writers in Israelite Christianity, as I said, Jesus finds ample representation as King-Messiah, but also as prophet and king, and, furthermore, as perfect priest and sacrifice, and always as sage, wise teacher, and rabbi. That accounts for the fact that the bulk of the ethical sayings given to him are commonplaces in the Judaism of the age. Accordingly, none of the symbolic systems at hand, with their associated modes of piety and faith and religious imagination, ever existed as we treat them, pure and unalloyed. For they were not ideal types awaiting description and interpretation.

The inquiry at hand centers on the symbols through which Jews expressed their feelings for God, their view of God's rule of the world, their own nation, and the lives they led. These symbols further embody and expose the way of life led by diverse groups of Jews, allowing us to grasp as a whole a sizable number of details about how things were done or not done. To seek a typology of the modes of piety, we look for the generative symbol of each of those modes: an altar, for the priestly ideal; a scroll of Scripture, for the ideal of wisdom; a coin marked "Israel's freedom: Year One" for the messianic modality. In each of these visual symbols we perceive the things we cannot touch, the hearts and minds we can only hope to evoke. Our supposition is that we enter into the imagination of someone else, long ago and far away, by our effort to appreciate and understand the way in which that other person framed the world, captured everything in some one thing: the sheep for the sacrifice, the memorized wise saying for the disciple, the stout heart for God's soldiers of light.

Priest, sage, soldier—all of these figures stand for Israel, or, rather, part of the nation. When all would meld into one, that one would stand for the formation of a system of fresh and unprecedented Judaism. Jesus represented as perfect priest, rabbi, Messiah was one such protean figure. The talmudic rabbi as Torah incarnate, priest manqué, and model of the son of David was another. In both cases we find a fresh reading of an old symbol, and, more important, an unprecedented rereading of established symbols in fresh and striking ways.

TYPES AND EXPRESSIVE SYMBOLS

The history of piety in Israel is the story of the successive arrangements and revisions of available symbols. From ancient Israelite times onward, there would be no new classification beyond these three categories or taxa. But no category would ever be left intact for long. When Jesus asked people what they thought he was, the enigmatic answer proved less interesting than the question. For the task he set before them was to reframe everything they knew in the encounter with the one they did not know. It was a labor of classification. When, along these same lines, the rabbis of the later centuries of late antiquity rewrote in their own images and likenesses the entire Scripture and history of Israel, dropping whole eras as though they had never been, ignoring vast bodies of old Jewish writing, inventing whole new books for the canon of Judaism, they did the same. They reworked the received in light of what they proposed to give. No mode of piety could be left untouched, for all proved promising. But every mode of piety would be reworked in light of the vast public events represented by the religious revolutionaries at hand: rabbi-clerks, rabbi-priests, rabbi-Messiah.

The issues of the symbols under discussion—Temple altar, sacred scroll, victory wreath for the head of the King-Messiah—addressed Jewish society at large. We need not reduce them to their social dimensions to recognize that, at the foundations, we deal with the issues of the organization of society and the selection and interpretation of its history. Let us rapidly review the sectors of society addressed by framers of these symbols.

The priest viewed society as organized through lines of structure emanating from the Temple. His caste stood at the top of a social scale in which all things were properly organized, each with its correct name and place. The sanctity inhering in Israel, the people, came to its richest embodiment in him, the priest. Food set aside for his rations at God's command possessed that same sanctity; so too did the table at which he ate his food, when properly protected. To the priest the sacred society of Israel produced no history, except for what happened in or to the Temple.

To the sage, the ongoing life of society demanded wise regulation. Relationships among people, guided by the laws and rules revealed of old and embodied in the Torah and best interpreted by the sage, were there to govern. Accordingly, the task of Israel was to construct a way of life in accordance with the revealed rules of the Torah. The sage, master of the rules, stood at the head.

So far as prophecy's insistence that the fate of the nation depended upon the faith and moral condition of society, history testified to the context and inner condition of Israel, viewed whole. Both sage and priest saw Israel from the aspect of eternity. But the nation lived out its life in this world, among other people coveting the very same land, within the politics of empires. The Messiah's kingship would resolve the issues of Israel's subordinated relationship to other nations and empires, establishing once for all time the correct context for priest and sage alike.

Implicit within the messianic framework was the perspective on a world out there for which priest and sage cared not at all—a society, nation, history. The priest saw the receding distances of the world beyond the Temple as less holy, then unholy, then unclean. All lands outside of the Land of Israel were chronically unclean with a corpse's uncleanness. All peoples but Israel were inherently unclean as corpses were unclean. Accordingly, life abided within Israel, and, in Israel, within the Temple. Outside, in the far distance, were the vacant lands and dead peoples, all of them an undifferentiated wilderness. From such a perspective on the world, no doctrine of Israel among the nations, no interest in the history of Israel and in the meaning of its past and future were apt to emerge.

The sagacity of the sage, in general, pertained to the streets, marketplaces, and domestic establishments—the household units—of Israel. What the sage said was wise, therefore wise as much for gentiles as for Israel. Wisdom in the nature of things proved international, moving easily across boundaries of culture and language, from eastern to southern to western Asia. Its focus, by definition, lay upon universal human experience, hence undifferentiated by nation, essentially unaffected by the large movements of history. Wisdom spoke about fathers and sons, masters and disciples, families and villages, not about nations, armies, and destiny. To be sure, sages spoke to and about Israel in particular.

So I suppose that, because of their diversity, the three principal motifs of Israelite existence might readily cohere. Each focused upon a distinct and particular aspect of the national life, so none essentially intersected with, or contradicted, any other. One could worship at the Temple, study the Torah, and fight in the army of the Messiah, and many did all three. Yet we must see these modes of being, and their consequent motifs of piety, as separate, each with its own potentiality of full realization wholly without the others.

For the three modes of human existence expressed in the symbolic systems of cult, Torah, and Messiah do demand choices. If one thing is important, then the others must be less important. History matters, or it happens "out there" and does not matter. The proper conduct of the cult determines the course of the seasons and the prosperity of the Land, or it is mere ritual. The Messiah will save Israel, or he will ruin everything. Accordingly, while we take for granted that people could live within the vision of priest, sage, and Messiah, we also recognize that it was a blurred perception. Narratives of the war of 66–73 C.E. emphasize how priests warned messianists not to endanger the Temple. Later sages—talmudic rabbis—paid slight honor to the messianic struggle led by Bar Kokba and after 70 C.E. claimed the right to tell priests what to do. It must follow that the way in which the several symbols are arranged and rearranged settles everything. Symbol change is social change. A mere amalgam of all three, by itself, hardly serves as a mirror for the mind of Israel. The way the three are bonded reflects an underlying human and social reality.

That is how it should be. Why? Because the three symbols, with their associated myths, the world-view they project, the way of life they define, stand for different views of what really matters in life. In investigating the existential foundations of the several symbolic systems available to ancient Jews, we seek to penetrate to the bedrock of Israel's reality, the basis for the life of the nation of Israel and each Israelite, the ground of being—even to the existential core we share with them.

HISTORY AND PRIVATE LIFE,
TIME AND ETERNITY

Let us unpack this notion of the two focuses of existence, public history and private home, hearth, society, and village. We may call the one "time," in that the focus of interest is in history, what happens day by day in the here and now. The other we may call "eternity," in that the focus of interest is in the ongoing patterns of life, birth and death, planting and harvest, the regular movement of the sun, moon, and stars in heaven, and of the night and day, Sabbaths and festivals, and regular seasons, on earth. The shared existential issue is this: How do we respond to the ups and downs of life? Every group that survives long enough experiences "history," those noteworthy events. The events of individual life, birth, maturing, marriage, death, do not make, or add up to, history, except for individuals. But the events of group-life formation of the group, developing social norms and patterns, depression or prosperity, war or peace—these do make history. When a small people coalesces and begins its course through history in the face of adversity, two things can happen.

Either the group disintegrates in the face of disaster, loses its hold on its individual members.

Or the group fuses and is strengthened by trial, is able to turn adversity into the occasion of renewal.

The triple focuses around which human and national existence were interpreted—priests', sages', and those of messianists or prophets, and apocalyptists'—emerge, we must remember, from the national and social consciousness of ancient Israel. The heritage of the Tanakh, the Hebrew Scriptures or "Old Testament," was carried forward among all three approaches to Judaism. The Jewish people has known the mystery of how to endure through history, for it is one of the oldest peoples now alive on the face of the earth. Even in ancient Israel, adversity elicited self-conscious response. Things did not merely *happen* to the ancient Israelites. Events were shaped, reformed, and interpreted by them, made into the raw materials for a renewal of the life of the group. The reason is that the ancient Israelites regarded their history as important, as teaching significant lessons. History was not merely "one damn thing after another." It had a purpose and was moving somewhere. The writers of Leviticus and Deuteronomy, of the historical books from Joshua through Kings, and of the prophetic literature agreed that, when Israel does God's will, its people enjoy times of peace, security, and prosperity, and when they do not, they are punished at the hands of mighty kingdoms, themselves raised up as instruments of God's wrath. This conception of the meaning of Israel's life produced a further question: How long? When do the great events of time come to their climax and conclusion? And in answer to that question, the hope for the Messiah, the anointed of God who would redeem the people and set them on the right path forever, thus ending the vicissitudes of history, was born.

Now, when we reach the first century C.E., we come to a turning point in the messianic hope. No one who knows the Gospels will be surprised to learn of the intense, vivid, prevailing expectation that the Messiah was coming soon. And it is hardly astonishing that that should be the case. For people who fix their attention on everyday events of world-shaking dimensions naturally will look forward to a better future. Given the Romans' conquest of the Land of Israel and appointment of a native king as ruler, we should not be surprised that people in some places looked forward to apocalyptic changes in Israel's future, such as had just now taken place.

What is surprising is the development of a second, quite different response to history. It is the response of people prepared once and for all to transcend everyday events, to take their leave of wars and rumors of wars, of politics and public life, and to attempt to construct a new reality above history, a way of viewing reality on the far side of everyday life. At hand after 70 C.E. was not merely a craven or exhausted passivity in the face of world-shaking events. We witness the beginnings of the active construction of a new mode of being. The decision is to exercise freedom. What that meant was to reconstruct conceptions of the meaning and ultimate significance of what happens without reference of history. It is a seeking of a world, not outside this one, but different from and better than the one formed by ordinary history. The second approach is a quest for eternity in the here and now, an effort to form a society capable of abiding amid change and storm. Indeed, it is a fresh reading of the meaning of history: The nations of the world make history and think what they do matters. But Israel knows that it is God who makes history, and it is the reality formed in response to God's will which *is* history.

That reality, that conception of time and change, forms the focus and the vision of the priestly tradition, continuing later in rabbinic Judaism. This sort of Judaism is essentially a metahistorical approach to life. It expresses an intense inwardness, and lays its stress upon the ultimate meaning contained within small and humble affairs. Rabbinic Judaism in time to come would set itself up as the alternative to all the forms of messianic Judaism whether leading to Christianity or to militaristic Zealotry and nationalism—that claimed to know the secret of history: the time of, and way to, redemption.

This approach to the life of Israel, stressing continuity and pattern and promising change only at the end, represents the union of two trends, as I have stressed. The one was symbolized by the altar, the other by the scroll of the Torah: the priest and the sage. In actual fact, the union was effected by a *kind* of priest-manqué, and a *kind* of sage. The former was the Pharisee (whom we meet in chapter 3), the latter, the scribe; the former, a particular sect of people who pretended, at home, that they were priests in the Temple. The latter was the scribe, member not of a sect but of a profession. The scribes were a class of teachers of the Torah, petty officials, and bureaucrats. The scribes knew and taught Torah. They took their interpretation of Torah very seriously, it goes without saying, and the act of study to them was of special importance. The Pharisees had developed, for their part, a peculiar perception of how to live and interpret life, which we may call an "as if" perception. In very specific ways the Pharisees claimed to live as if they were priests, as if they had to obey at home the laws that applied to the Temple. When the Temple itself was destroyed, it turned out that the Pharisees had prepared for that tremendous change in the sacred economy. They continued to live as if—as if the Temple stood, as if there was a new Temple formed of the Jewish people. Joined to their mode of looking at life was the substance of the scribal ideal, the stress on learning of Torah and carrying out its teachings. And, in time to come, the later rabbis would take over the prophetic heritage as well.

These, then, represent the alternatives to how great events were to be experienced and understood. One was the historical-messianic way, stressing the importance of those events and concentrating upon their weight and meaning. The other was the metahistorical, priestly-rabbinic way, laying emphasis upon the transcendence of events and the construction of an eternal, changeless mode of being, capable of riding out the waves of history.

SALVATION VS. SANCTIFICATION

Accordingly, once we have identified the principal strands of Judaic consciousness, we deal with two questions.

First, what made one focus—the priestly and the sagacious, or the messianic trend—appear to people to be more compelling and consequential than another? The answer becomes obvious when we realize that each kind of piety addresses its own point of concern. The several of them speak about different things to different people. We may sort them out from one another if we return to an earlier observation. Priests and sages turn inward, toward the concrete everyday life of the community. Messianists and their prophetic and apocalyptic teachers turn outward, toward the affairs of states and nations. Priests see the world of life in Israel, death, beyond. They know what happens to Israel, requiring no theory about the place of Israel among the nations. The nations, as we noticed, form an undifferentiated realm of death. Sages, all the more, speak of home and hearth, fathers and sons, husbands and wives, the village and enduring patterns of life within it. What place in this domestic scheme for the realities of history—wars and threats of war, the rise and fall of empires, encompassing the consciousness of a singular society amidst other societies?

Second, what draws the three focuses together and makes them one? It was an event in which all are equally involved. This was important to those to whom great events of history appear momentous, but also beyond the (even feigned) act of ignoring history deliberately committed by priests and sages. Such an event proved paramount in the period at hand. The ultimate destruction of the Temple in 70 C.E. provided the catalyst that joined priest, sage, and, in time to come, messianist, thereby creating that amalgam that was the Judaism framed by the rabbis of the Mishnah and collections of *midrashim* and two Talmuds. The three definitive components were then bonded.

The principle that Judaism would constitute a way of life aimed at sanctification was contributed by the priestly trend.

The notion that Judaism demanded a life of study of Torah and the application of Torah to the life of the community derived from the scribes.

The conception that the community of Israel stood apart from the nations and lived out a destiny of its own was the gift of the prophetic, apocalyptic, messianic trend.

Events then added up to history. The history of Israel was shaped by God's response to Israel's study of Torah and life of sanctification. When the whole came together, forming the perfect creation as at the beginning, then would come the last and enduring Sabbath, counterpart to the Sabbath of creation: the Messiah and his age.

So the single critical event of the age presented a crisis of the priestly caste, the sages' profession, and the political and messianic sectors of the nation alike. The decisive event, cutting across all classes and movements of history, the caesura of the life of the cult, the classroom, and the clerks of government alike, was the destruction of the Temple of Jerusalem in 70 C.E. What was important was not that the Temple was destroyed; that had happened not once but many times before. It was that the Temple was not then rebuilt.

In 586 B.C.E. the Jerusalem Temple had fallen, but a scant three generations had to pass before it was rebuilt. From that time onward, whatever happened to the Temple building, the cult endured. So the entire history of Israel testified to the Temple's prominence in the world of Israel. If it should again be destroyed, then, following the established pattern, people had every reason to expect it would be rebuilt. Accordingly, the fact of the destruction in 70 C.E., while bearing profound consequences, by itself merely raised a question. The calamity that, three generations later Bar Kokba's armies, intent on retaking the holy city and rebuilding the Temple, suffered total defeat, turned the question into a crisis, the earlier destruction into the decisive turning point. But in what direction? And, more important, with what meaning for the whole of the past of Israel? The answer, stated very briefly, is simple. In the aftermath of the cultic, political, military disaster of 70 and 135 C.E., everything would be reworked, the entire heritage revised and renewed.

So in the later first and second centuries the diverse varieties of Judaic piety present in Israel before 70 C.E. came to bonding in a new and wholly unprecedented way, with each party to the union imposing its logic upon the other constituents of the whole. The ancient categories remained. But they were so profoundly revised and transformed that nothing was preserved intact. Judaism as we know it, the Judaism of Scripture and Mishnah, midrash and Talmud, thereby effected the ultimate transvaluation of all the values, of all the kinds of Judaism that had come before, from remote Israelite times onward. Through the person and figure of the rabbi, the whole burden of Israel's heritage was taken up, renewed, handed on, from late antiquity to the present day.

3

THE
PHARISEES

The Pharisees are important for two reasons. First, the Gospels portray them as one of the principal opposition groups to Jesus. Second, Judaism as we know it generally traces its roots back to the Pharisees. How so? The Mishnah, the first great document of Judaism in its normative form, ca. 200 C.E., includes teachings attributed to authorities known to us from other sources to be Pharisees. These are, in particular, Gamaliel and his son, Simeon. The Mishnah, moreover, regards Gamaliel's father, the great rabbi Hillel, as one of the chief authorities for the Mishnah's own traditions. It follows that, long after the period at hand, the Mishnah preserved teachings allegedly belonging to the Pharisees in the time of Jesus.

Describing the Pharisees is not easy. The reason is that when people describe that rather small group, they pass their opinion also on large issues of our own day. Jews tend to praise the Pharisees as the source of wisdom and learning, because, as I said, Jews also claim to trace their religious traditions to the Pharisees. Christians today violently attack Pharisees. Protestants emphasize the legalism of the Pharisees, another way of attacking what they conceive to be the legalism of the Roman Catholic communion. Catholics simply draw upon well-known judgments in the Gospels themselves, which portray the Pharisees as hypocrites. But often many Protestants and Catholics, speaking of the Pharisees of long ago, really mean ("perfidious") Judaism of today. Consequently, it is unusually difficult to take up the Pharisees with that attitude of reasoned curiosity that makes learning a source of light. The best we can do is describe the sources of such information as we have about the group at hand.

THE SOURCES

What do we know about the Pharisees before the destruction of Jerusalem in 70 C.E.? More important, how do we know anything about them at all?

We have three separate bodies of information: first, the historical narratives of Josephus, a Jewish historian who, between 75 and ca. 100 C.E., wrote the history of the Jews from the beginnings to the destruction of Jerusalem, including the war against Rome which had led to the destruction; second, biographical traditions about, and sayings attributed to, Jesus, assembled in the nascent Christian community between ca. 50 and ca. 90 C.E.; third, the laws and sayings attributed to pre-70 C.E. Pharisees by their successors and heirs, the rabbis of late first- and second-century Palestine.

1. Josephus's narrative requires interpretation in the light of his own life in Roman politics after 70 C.E.

2. The Gospels' traditions about the Pharisees show little interest in the Pharisees, except as a convenient basis for polemic or narrative. Information about the Pharisees which the Gospel narrators had to have known for their own purposes consisted of two significant facts: Pharisaic stress on tithing, and Pharisaic commitment to keeping the purity laws outside of the Temple. But the Gospels' superficial knowledge of the details of what the Pharisees actually did hardly suggests much interest in the Pharisaic set in its own terms.

3. The rabbinical traditions about the Pharisees prove most complex of all. The legal materials, attested shortly after 70 C.E., all are reworked in the forms used after. The rabbinical history of Pharisaism, moreover, turns out to be strikingly relevant to the spiritual crisis in the aftermath of the Bar Kokba War.

These separate sources furthermore are quite different in character. The first is a systematic, coherent historical narrative. The second is a well-edited collection of stories and sayings. The third consists chiefly of laws, arranged by legal categories in codes, and commentaries on those codes. Moreover, the purposes of the authors or compilers of the respective collections differ from one other.

1. Josephus was engaged in explaining to the Jewish world of his day that Rome was not at fault for the destruction of the Temple, and in telling the Roman world that the Jewish people had been misled, and therefore were not to be held responsible for the terrible war.

2. The interest of the Gospels is not in the history of the Jewish

people, but in the life and teachings of Jesus, to which that history supplies background.

3. The rabbinical legislators show no keen interest in narrative, biographical, or historical problems, but take as their task the promulgation of laws for the government and administration of the Jewish community.

The historical question we bring to the sources would have been remote and incomprehensible to all three. We want to know what really happened. How accurate are our sources? Our measure of accuracy is historical reality. To what historical situation does a story testify? What apologetic or polemical purposes are reflected in the narrative? What is the history of a saying or story? Whose interest does it serve? What case does it help to make? We thus begin with a skepticism that does not characterize the ancient sources, and we are not perturbed by fundamentally negative results.

Much that we are told about the Pharisees reflects the situation, interests, and viewpoint of the teller, not of the historical Pharisees. The historical enterprise therefore promises modest results, for all we know about the historical Pharisees consists in what three interested parties have to tell us, which is in turn shaped by their beliefs and concerns. But that is always the difficulty in the study of the history of religious movements and leaders around whose teachings later controversies tend to focus, and to whose authority later disputes are referred. The study of the historical Pharisees therefore serves to illustrate a commonplace methodological difficulty. Consideration of these sometimes difficult sources may provide useful experience in analyzing other historical-religious sources as well.

IN THE AFTERMATH OF DISASTER

The single most important event in the history of Judaism from the destruction of the Temple by the Babylonians in 587 B.C.E. to the conquest of Palestine by the Arabs in ca. 640 C.E. was the destruction of the Second Temple by the Romans in 70 C.E.

It was decisive not only because the political basis of Jewish community life had rested on the Temple government, but also because the religious life of the people had centered on the sacrificial cult. To be sure, small groups tended to refocus their life away from, and in opposition to, the Temple. But for the mass, the Temple represented the nexus between heaven and earth. God had revealed his will in the Torah—the revelation to Moses at Sinai—which contained numerous cultic laws. Those laws were kept in the Temple, where the daily sacrifices and the exact sacrificial technology represented a primary means by which Israel served its father in heaven. Destruction of the Second Temple therefore provided the point of contention for all parties who, in the aftermath, claimed to tell the Jews the meaning of the recent unhappy events and the way in which they now should live.

Some of the several sources concerning pre-70 Pharisaic Judaism were shaped in response to the crisis of 70 C.E. With the Temple in ruins it was important to preserve and, especially, to interpret the record of what had gone before. Josephus tells the story of the people and the great war. For their part, the Gospels record the (to the Christians) climactic moment in Israel's supernatural life, without much sustained interest in the destruction of the Temple. But it formed part of the facts to be dealt with. The rabbis describe the party to which they traced their origin, and through which they claimed to reach back to the authority of Moses at Sinai. The issue in all three cases was: What is the meaning of the decisive history just passed—whether in the life of Christ or in the life of Israel?

1. To Josephus the answer is that Israel's welfare depends upon obedience to the laws of the Torah as expounded by the Pharisees and upon peaceful relationships with Rome.

2. The Gospels claim that, with the coming of the Messiah, the Temple ceased to enjoy its former importance, and those who had had charge of Israel's life—chief among them the priests, scribes, and Pharisees—were shown through their disbelief to have ignored the hour of their salvation. Their unbelief is explained in part by the Pharisees' hypocrisy and self-seeking.

3. The rabbis contend that the continuity of the mosaic Torah is unbroken. Destruction of the Temple, while lamentable, does not mean Israel has lost all means of service to the Creator. The way of the Pharisees leads, without break, back to Sinai and forward to the rabbinical circle reforming at Yavneh. The Oral Torah revealed by Moses and handed on from prophet to scribe, sage, and rabbi remains in the hands of Israel. The legal record of pre-70 Pharisaism requires careful preservation because it remains wholly in effect.

THEOLOGY

The theological side to Pharisaic Judaism before 70 C.E., however, is not easily accessible, for the pre-70 beliefs, ideas, and values have been taken over and revised by the rabbinical masters after that time. We therefore cannot reliably claim that an idea first known to us in a later rabbinical document, from the third century and afterward, was originally both known and understood in the same way. For now, the only reliable information derives from Josephus, the Gospels, and rabbinical literature, beginning with the Mishnah, the law code of Judah the Patriarch. As is clear, none of these gives an accurate account of Pharisaic theology before 70 C.E. Josephus concentrates on political questions, and the theological teachings to which he does allude are primarily of a general philosophical character. The Gospels have no interest in Pharisaic theology, and rabbinical attributions of theological sayings to the Pharisaic masters before 70, which are not likely to be reliable, constitute little more than a collection of sage comments, commonplaces of practical wisdom. We shall see some of these in chapter 4.

POLEMICS

The historical task is made still more complicated by the long history of abuse to which the Pharisees have been subjected in Western civilization. The New Testament's negative picture was widely reproduced in Christian preaching, writing, and scholarship. To the present day one will find the Pharisees described in exactly the polemical spirit of the Gospels, as if the synoptic writers had intended to write an objective, critical history, not a highly partisan carica-ture. "Pharisee" became a synonym for hypocrite, and "Pharisaic" for formalism or self-righteousness. Thus these definitions (*Shorter Oxford English Dictionary*, 3d rev. ed. [Oxford: At the Clarendon Press, 1955], 1485–86):

Pharisaic: Resembling the Pharisees in being strict in doctrine and ritual, without the spirit of piety; laying stress upon the outward show of re-ligion and morality, and assuming superiority on that account; hypo-critical; formal; self-righteous.

Pharisaism: The character and spirit of the Pharisees; hypocrisy; formal-ism; self-righteousness.

Pharisee: One of an ancient Jewish sect distinguished by their strict ob-servance of the traditional and written law, and by their pretensions to superior sanctity. A person of this disposition; a self-righteous person; a formalist; a hypocrite.

Lexicography in the service of an anti-Judaic Christian theology thus accurately reproduces the polemic of the Gospels.

These definitions of Pharisee and Pharisaic are part of the cultural background of the West, an aspect of the anti-Semitism nurtured by Christian theology of a certain sort. They cannot be allowed to influence the issues of our inquiry. We want to get behind these cultural artifacts, which are unrelated to the historical task.

Naturally, on the Jewish side, a contrary polemic was not lacking. Since rabbinical traditions contain numerous stories and sayings attributed to Pharisaic masters of the period before 70 C.E., it was easy for Jewish scholarship to demonstrate not only the theological animus, but also the historical incompetence of those Christian scholars of ancient and modern times who ignored important parts of the Pharisaic record. Hillel, a near-contemporary of Jesus, and the most important figure in pre-70 Pharisaism according to the rabbinical traditions, is credited with the aphorism, "What is hateful to yourself, do not do to your neighbor. That is the entire Torah. All the rest is commentary. Now go forth and learn." He is also made to say, "If I am not for myself, who will be for me? But when I am for myself, what am I? And if not now, when?" These and similar sayings are routinely cited as evidence that Pharisees were not hypocrites, formalists, or self-righteous men.

WHO WERE THE PHARISEES?
JOSEPHUS'S ANSWER

At the outset of our inquiry it is best that we seek perspective on the Pharisaic sect in its own setting. Josephus tells us that "more than six thousand Pharisees" refused to take an oath of loyalty to Herod:

> There was also a group of Jews priding itself on its adherence to ancestral custom and claiming to observe the laws of which the Deity approves, and by these men, called Pharisees, the women of the court [of Herod] were ruled. These men were able to help the king greatly because of their foresight, and yet they were obviously intent upon combating and injuring him. At last when the whole Jewish people affirmed by an oath that it would be loyal to Caesar and to the king's government, these men, over six thousand in number, refused to take this oath, and when the king punished them with a fine, Pheroras' wife paid the fine for them. In return for her friendliness they foretold—for they were believed to have foreknowledge of things through God's appearances to them—that by God's decree Herod's throne would be taken from him, both from himself and his descendants, and the royal power would fall to her and Pherora and to any children that they might have. (Josephus, *Jewish Antiquities* 17:41–4, trans. Ralph Marcus [Cambridge, Mass.: Harvard Univ. Press, 1963], 391, 393)

What was the position of these six thousand Pharisees in relationship to the mass of the Jewish population?

Morton Smith, the great historian of antiquity, points out that the man who was a Pharisee was not primarily a Pharisee all the time. He presumably played many roles in society. Gamaliel is described in Acts 5:34 as a Pharisee in the council of the Temple. Was he appointed to the council because he was a Pharisee, and thus represented the party or sect there? Or was he a Pharisee who also happened for some other reason, perhaps social distinction or political and economic power, to be appointed in the Temple? Was he then a Temple councilor who also happened to be a Pharisee? What was the meaning of "being a Pharisee" in the lives of various sorts of people? It seems most likely that to be a Pharisee was not a profession, but an avocation. Pharisaism was, in terms of ancient civilization, a sect within the "philosophy" of Judaism. Smith stresses:

> Judaism to the ancient world was a philosophy. That world had no general term for *religion*. It could speak of a particular system of rites (a cult or an initiation), or a particular set of beliefs (doctrines or opinions), or a legal code, or a body of national customs or traditions; but for the peculiar synthesis of all these which we call a "religion," the one Hellenistic word which came closest was "philosophy." So when Judaism first took shape and became conscious of itself and its own peculiarity in the Hellenized world of the later Persian Empire, it described itself with the Hellenic term meaning the wisdom of its people (Deut. 4:6). To the success of this concept within Judaism the long roll call of the wisdom literature bears witness. Further, the claim was accepted by the surrounding world. To those who admired Judaism it was "the cult of wisdom" (for so we should translate the word "philosophy" which they used to describe it), and to those who disliked it, it was "atheism," which is simply the other side of the coin, the regular term of abuse applied to philosophy by its opponents. (Morton Smith, "Palestinian Judaism in the First Century," in *Israel: Its Role in Civilization*, ed. Moshe David [New York: Harper & Brothers, 1956], 67–81)

The Pharisees claimed to be authoritative because they taught a philosophy that derived from Moses at Sinai. They therefore preserved a "chain of tradition" reaching back from their own day to the authority of remote antiquity. Their piety was centered on the revelation of Moses. Smith says:

> It is . . . not surprising that Jews living, as Palestinian Jews did, in the Greco-Roman world, and thinking of their religion as the practice of wisdom, should think of the groups in their society which were distinguished by peculiar theories and practices as different schools of the na-

tional philosophy. (Smith, "Palestinian Judaism in the First Century," 79–80)

THE PHARISEES AS HELLENISTS

Thus Palestinian Judaism overall, and the Pharisaic sect in particular, are to be seen as Jewish modes of a common, international cultural "style" known as Hellenism. To see Palestinian Judaism outside of its context within world civilization is to misinterpret the meaning of its accomplishments. The Jews were not an isolated or provincial people, and their "philosophy" was not incomprehensible, at least in form, to the rest of civilized humankind. The Jews, on the contrary, responded to the challenge of Hellenism by shaping a uniquely Jewish form of that common culture. Nor was this merely in generalities. The Pharisees, for one, exhibited numerous traits familiar to Hellenistic culture, as Smith points out:

> Not only was the theory of the Pharisaic school that of a school of Greek philosophy, but so were its practices. Its teachers taught without pay, like philosophers; they attached to themselves particular disciples who followed them around and served them, like philosophers; they looked to gifts for support, like philosophers; they were exempt from taxation, like philosophers; they were distinguished in the street by their walk, speech, and peculiar clothing, like philosophers; they practiced and praised asceticism, like philosophers; and finally—what is, after all, the meat of the matter—they discussed the questions philosophers discussed and reached the conclusions philosophers reached. . . .

> If there was any such thing, then, as an "orthodox Judaism," it must have been that which is now almost unknown to us, the religion of the average "people of the land." But the different parts of the country were so different, such gulfs of feeling and practice separated Idumea, Judea, Caesarea, and Galilee, that even on this level there was probably no more agreement between them than between any one of them and a similar area in the Diaspora. And in addition to the local differences, the country swarmed with special sects, each devoted to its own tradition. Some of these, the followings of particular prophets, may have been spontaneous revivals of Israelite religion as simple as anything in Judges. But even what little we know of these prophets suggests that some of them, at least, taught a complex theology. As for the major philosophic sects—the Pharisees, Sadducees, and Essenes—the largest and ultimately the most influential of them, the Pharisees, numbered only about 6,000, had not real hold either on the government or on the masses of the people, and was, as were the others, profoundly Hellenized.

This period of Palestinian Jewish history, then, is the successor to one marked by great receptivity to outside influences. It is itself characterized by original developments of those influences. These developments, by their variety, vigor, and eventual significance, made this small country during this brief period the seedbed of the subsequent religious history of the Western world. (Smith, "Palestinian Judaism in the First Century," 81.)

We learn from Smith's characterization that the Pharisees were a small group within Palestinian Judaism, a philosophical school with a particular set of beliefs and religious practices. They claimed the right to rule all the Jews by virtue of their possessing the "Oral Torah" of Moses, that is, the body of traditions not written in Scriptures, but revealed to Moses at Mount Sinai along with the written Torah. They referred to a list of masters extending back to Moses, whom they later called "our rabbi." In their own setting, however, the Pharisees were much like any other Hellenistic philosophical school or sect.

THE TWO PICTURES OF THE PHARISEES

Let us now return to the sources themselves. The simple fact is that there is a striking discontinuity among the three principal sources which speak of the Pharisees before 70 C.E. To state matters simply: What Josephus thinks characteristic of the Pharisees are matters which play little or no role in what Mark and Matthew regard as significant, and what the later rabbis think the Pharisees said is congruent in theme to the picture of Q, Mark, and Matthew but scarcely intersects with the topics and themes important to Josephus. In this regard, the picture drawn by Matthew and Mark and that drawn by the later rabbis are essentially coherent, and together differ from the portrait left to us by Josephus.

More specifically, if we construct the agenda of Pharisaic traditions we should have expected on the basis of external descriptions of the sect, we discern a remarkable disparity. The traits of Pharisaism emphasized by Josephus, their principal beliefs and practices, nowhere occur in the rabbinic traditions of the Pharisees. The issues important to other sects of the period before 70 C.E., those problems that occupied the attention of the authorities and a central place in the traditions of the Christians and Qumranians, and of the writers of Apocryphal and Pseudepigraphic literature and related collections, simply do not come to the surface in the rabbinic traditions about the Pharisees.

THE RABBINIC TRADITIONS
ABOUT THE PHARISEES

The focus of interest of the rabbinic traditions about the Pharisees is the internal affairs of the Pharisaic party itself. The primary partisan issues center upon Shammai's and his House's relationship to Hillel and his House or disciple circle. The competing sects, by contrast, are ignored. Essenes and Christians make no appearance at all. The Romans never occur. The Hasmonean monarchy is reduced to a single name, Yannai the King, for Yohanan the High Priest, who, so far as the rabbinic traditions about the Pharisees are concerned, was a good Pharisee. In all, the traditions give the impression of intense concentration on the inner life of the party, or sect, whose intimate affairs take precedence, in the larger scheme of history, over the affairs of state, cult, and country. The state is a shadowy presence at best. The cult is of secondary importance. The country's life and the struggle with Rome as a whole are bypassed in silence. What we have, therefore, are the records of the party chiefly in regard to the life of the party itself.

When we compare what Josephus says about the Pharisees to what the later rabbinic traditions have to say, there is scarcely a point of contact, let alone intersection. Josephus says next to nothing about the predominant issues in the rabbinic traditions about the Pharisees. Shammai and Hillel are not explicitly mentioned, let alone their Houses. Above all, we find not the slightest allusion to laws of ritual purity, agricultural taboos, Sabbath and festivals, and the like, which predominate in the traditions of the Houses. We could not, relying upon Josephus, recover a single significant detail of the rabbinic traditions about the Pharisees, let alone the main outlines of the whole.

THE GOSPELS' PHARISEES

When we survey the references to Pharisees in the Synoptic Gospels, we observe close correspondences to what the later rabbinic traditions say. While the synoptic writers have no knowledge of the Houses of Shammai and Hillel, which ought to have been important in the period with which they deal, but assuredly were important in the period in which they wrote, they do lay emphasis on matters familiar in the rabbinic traditions. As we review the recurrent themes in the Gospels' accounts of the Pharisees, we find the following: Sabbath observance, in particular, picking food and healing the sick; cleanness laws, in particular the view that cleanness laws are less important than ethical commandments, and in the same context, eating with people who do not keep either cleanness laws or ethical commandments (tax collectors and the like); consecrating objects to the Temple and oath-taking; stress on tithing little things and (again) neglecting ethical matters; fasting; and lawful divorce.

To the legal agenda, we may add doctrinal questions: the character and power of the Son of Man; the value of baptism; signs as authentication of the Messiah; relations to the Roman government; the resurrection of the dead, tied to a levirate pericope; and the relative value of the respective commandments. The third category consists of the abuse of Pharisees; this is of no concern here. The legal agenda at every point has a counterpart in the rabbinic traditions of the Pharisees. Moreover, the stress of the Gospels seems just about right: cleanness laws, agricultural taboos, Sabbath and festival observance, family laws. We further observed attention to Temple consecration and oaths. Only fasting seems to play no significant part in the rabbinic traditions about the Pharisees.

The doctrinal issues are quite another matter. We have no rabbinic traditions about the Pharisees concerning the Messiah, his powers, rights, and obligations. Were we to construct a picture of first-century Palestinian Judaism entirely on the basis of the rabbinic traditions about the Pharisees, we should not have known that the Messiah was a significant element. Indeed, we should not have heard of the messianic expectation at all. Baptism in the sense of the Gospels' discussion has not come before us, although baptism in another sense, primarily for the purification of ritual uncleanness, not in relationship to the forgiveness of sin, is of course well-attested. But these look like different baptisms; the one is primarily ritual, the other moral. The Gospels' tendency to ethicize both baptism and purity rules and to set tithing into opposition with moral behavior is polemical; but is not without precedent in biblical prophecy. No echo of that attitude toward ritual comes before us in the rabbinic traditions about the Pharisees. As we observed, the Romans nowhere make an appearance. Whether or not one should pay taxes is never raised in materials we have reviewed.

A wide range of issues important in the traditions concerning other groups, and of other groups concerning the Pharisees, is either entirely absent or strikingly subordinated in the rabbinic traditions about the Pharisees. Questions to which we find no answers in the rabbinic materials include the following: What was the canon of the

Scriptures? How did the Pharisees view other groups? Did the Pharisees believe in the immortality of the soul? What was the Pharisees' attitude to the Temple? to sacrifice? to the priesthood? What were the interpretations of baptism supplied by Pharisees? How did the Pharisees view heteropraxy and heterodoxy? Was the claim of being the Messiah taken seriously? Was it considered punishable? What were their attitudes to apocalyptic visions, ideas, and personalities? What was the attitude of the party toward Hellenistic society in general? Toward Greek-speaking Jews in particular? To what degree did the Pharisees at various stages in their history before 70 C.E. involve themselves in the politics of the country? When and why did they pursue an independent course, and when did they withdraw entirely from political life? What was the inner institutional structure of the Pharisaic party? How were people admitted and expelled? One could formulate a substantial agenda of questions, problems, and concerns important either to other sects, or to Jewish Palestine and its social and religious life as a whole. That agenda is unattended to by the rabbinic tradents, who, as I said, tell us about what primarily interested them. The shape of those interests, on the one side, and the configuration of the historical Pharisees, on the other, do not seem entirely congruent to one another.

POINTS IN COMMON: THE LAWS

Now that we have gained a measure of perspective upon the emphases of the rabbinical traditions about the Pharisees, we may select the one topic on which these sources are apt to be essentially sound, namely, the laws they impute to the figures before 70 C.E. who we believe were Pharisees. The congruity in the themes of the laws attributed to the Pharisees by both the Gospels and the later rabbinic sources seems to me striking. What it means is that, from speaking of traditions about the Pharisees, we are apt to address the historical Pharisees themselves in the decades before the destruction of the Temple in 70 C.E. The historical Pharisees in the decades before the destruction of Jerusalem are portrayed by legal traditions that seem to be fundamentally sound in theme, perhaps also in substance, and attested by references of masters who may reasonably be supposed to have known what they were talking about. Which laws pertained primarily to Pharisaism and which were part of the law common to all of Palestinian Jewry? Most of the laws before us, verified early or late, affect primarily the sectarian life of the party.

The laws that made a sect sectarian were those that either were interpreted and obeyed by the group in a way different from other groups or from common society at large, on the one hand, or were to begin with observed only by the group, on the other. In the latter category are the purity laws, which take so large a place in the Pharisaic corpus. One primary mark of Pharisaic commitment was the observance of the laws of ritual purity outside of the Temple, where everyone kept them. Eating one's secular, that is, unconsecrated, food in a state of ritual purity, as if one were a Temple priest in the cult, was one of the two significations of party membership. The manifold circumstances of everyday life required the multiplication of concrete rules. Representative of the former category may be the laws of tithing and other agricultural taboos. Here we are less certain. Pharisees clearly regarded keeping the agricultural rules as a primary religious duty. But whether, to what degree, and how other Jews did so is not clear. And the agricultural laws, just like the purity rules, in the end affected table-fellowship, namely, what one might eat.

The early Christian traditions on both points represent the Pharisees as reproaching Jesus because his followers did not keep these two kinds of laws at all, that is, why they were not Pharisees. The answer was that the primary concern was for ethics. Both the question and the answer are disingenuous. The questioners are represented as rebuking the Christians for not being Pharisees— which begs the question, for everyone presumably knew Christians were not Pharisees. The answer takes advantage of the polemical opening: Pharisees are not concerned with ethics, a point repeatedly made in the anti-Pharisaic pericopes, depending upon a supposed conflict between rules of table-fellowship, on the one side, and ethical behavior on the other. The obvious underlying claim is that Christian table-fellowship does not depend upon the sorts of rules important in the table-fellowship of other groups.

Since the tithes and offerings either went to the Levites and priests or had to be consumed in Jerusalem, and since the purity rules were to begin with Temple matters, we note that the Pharisees claimed laymen are better informed as to purity and Temple laws than the Temple priesthood. Morton Smith ("The Dead Sea Sect in Relation to Ancient Judaism," *New Testament Studies* 7 [1960] :347–60) observes, "Differences as to the interpretation of the purity laws and especially as to the consequent question of table fellowship were among the principal causes of the separation of Christianity from the rest of Judaism and the early fragmentation of Christianity itself. The same thing holds for the Qumran community, and, within Pharisaic tradition, the haburah. They are essentially groups whose members observe the same interpretation of the purity rules and therefore can have table fellowship with each other. It is no accident that the essential act of communion in all these groups is participation in common meals." Since food which had not been properly grown or tithed could not be eaten, and since the staple of the diet was agricultural products and not meat, the centrality of the agricultural rules in no small degree is on account of precisely the same consideration: What may one eat, and under what circumstances?

The commonplace character of Pharisaic table-fellowship is striking. The group's ordinary gatherings were not as a group at all, but in any private home, with all participating in an ordinary meal. All meals required ritual purity. Pharisaic table-fellowship took place in the same circumstance in which all nonritual table-fellowship occurred: common folk, eating everyday meals, in an everyday way, amid neighbors who were not members of the sect, and engaged in workaday pursuits like everyone else. This made the actual purity rules and food restrictions all the more important, for only they set the Pharisee apart from the people among whom he constantly lived. Since it was not on festivals or on Sabbaths alone, but on weekdays, in the towns, without the telling of myths or the reading of holy books (Torah talk at table is attested only later), or the reenactment of first or last things, Pharisaic table-fellowship depended solely on observance of the law. That observance, apart from the meal itself, was not marked off by benedictions or other rites. No stories were told during the meal or about it. Keeping the laws included few articulate statements, for example, blessings. The setting for observance was the field and the kitchen, the bed, and the street. The occasion for observance was set every time a person picked up a common nail or purchased a *seah* of wheat, by himself, without priests to bless his deed or sages to tell him what to do. So keeping the Pharisaic rule required neither an occasional, exceptional rite at, but external to, the meal, as in the Christian sect in Judaism, nor taking up residence in a monastic commune, as in the Qumranian sect in Judaism, but perpetual sanctification of daily life through rite, on the one side, and constant inner awareness of the communal order of being, on the other.

WOMEN AND PHARISAISM

Once the focus of piety through sanctification shifted out of the Temple, a new opportunity for women opened up. We recall that women had gained access only to the outer precincts of the Temple. They could never approach the altar; they could not do the things men could do. Even if they were members of the priestly caste, their standing in the Temple was exactly the same as that of the lowliest daughter of the subordinated castes, for instance, the child of a couple legally not permitted to marry. But with the emphasis upon observing the rules of cultic cleanness, hence eating food in holy meals not only in the Temple but also in the home, everything shifted. For all of the evidence of this period takes for granted that women prepared meals. Accordingly, women gained a central role in the correct observance of the rules governing cultic cleanness. Let us not miss the point: if you keep these rules, you eat your food as if you were a priest, so you enter the status of holiness. But women bore responsibility for preparing food in accordance with the taboos. It follows that women now enjoyed the power to secure sanctification—and this in the very context from which, in the Temple itself, they were excluded. The paradox is striking.

We should not miss the full dimensions of the enhanced position now available. First, women were expected to keep the same cultic taboos as men did. So they attained complete equality in the life of the rites of the home. So far as the rules at hand were concerned, there were no distinctions between men and women. Second, the status of women, so far as cultic holiness was concerned, did not depend upon their relationship to men. They were not going to be cultically clean because they were descended from a father who was a priest, or because they married a priest. If women were daughters of priests, they also did not lose their status as persons who might attain sanctification merely because they married someone of a lower caste than themselves. Consequently, in the Pharisaic rite women enjoyed full personhood. Their status depended wholly upon what they themselves did or did not do, upon rules applicable equally to women and to men.

On the other hand, keeping the rules of cultic cleanness meant that in a period in which a woman was "unclean," that is, menstruating, she could not prepare food that was to be eaten by people who observed the taboos. What this meant in practice was that women could not prepare meals for their families for about a week each month. The alternative was that during the wife's menstrual period, the family simply ate its ordinary food not in a condition of cultic cleanness at all. It was no sin, but it also represented a considerable comedown. To be sure, households encompassed more than the nuclear family; if one woman was menstruating, there were others to prepare the meals. The laws of cultic contamination, however, extended even to objects upon which unclean persons (such as are listed in Leviticus 15) stood, sat, or lay. Menstruating women therefore had to take special care to demarcate the places in which they walked, sat, and stood during a week each month.

In all, the importance of the woman was emphasized in Pharisaism. But it also complicated her everyday life. While ordinary Jewish couples, who did not think the rules of cultic cleanness applied outside of the Temple, refrained from having sexual relations when the women were menstruating, the sexual taboo cannot have imposed so broad a range of inconveniences as did the sectarian ones at hand. How women responded we do not know. We do have ample evidence that women as much as men voluntarily undertook the disciplines of sanctification as Pharisees understood them. But whatever writing we have comes from men only. So the picture, as usual, is incomplete.

CONCLUSION

The debate on the Pharisees embodies the Christian critique of Judaism, and the Jews' apologetic for their religion. The debate tends to be framed in polemical terms on both sides. Quite naturally, the negative picture of the Pharisees as legalists, hypocrites, people who care for the form but not the spirit of the law, predominates in Western culture. To be called "a Pharisee" is no compliment. The other side insists, in exactly these same terms, that Pharisees really preached a religion of love, citing sources out of the whole of rabbinic literature to prove it. For Jews know that it is their observance of the living faith, so rich in concrete expressions in ordinary life, that is under attack.

What happens, however, if the issue may be drawn differently? Then the debate falls away, since it misses the real point of both the Pharisees and their early Christian enemies and critics. In fact we have the picture of two sets of Jews—the ones for whom the Gospels speak, on the one side, and the ones described in the laws assigned to authorities before 70 C.E. in the later rabbinic writings, on the other side—who really are talking about different things and therefore are unable to address the important issues in common.

Clearly, the invective of the Gospels against the Pharisees bespeaks competition and strife between the communities for whom the Gospels speak and this other, quite separate, community of Israelites. To the framers of the Gospels, salvation is at hand. Equally obvious, the stress of the Pharisees on the minutiae of cultic law, observed even outside of the cult, expresses a profound yearning for sanctification by participation in the holy and eternal life of the Temple. Now so far as salvation and sanctification talk of different things to different people, there really is no debate between Christian and Jew on the character of the Pharisees, and no apologetic is needed. Understanding supersedes dispute, respect for the deepest concern of the other takes the place of the need to justify and defend oneself. An issue between the Pharisees as we know them in rabbinical writings and the Christian critics of the Pharisees as we know their views in sayings assigned to Jesus is a simple question of how salvation is to be attained. That question endures, although in this very different century of ours the old bitterness is gone and a new sense of shared humility before God flourishes.

4
THE FIGURE
OF
HILLEL

When we take up the question of the Pharisees, we focus attention on Hillel in particular because he was the greatest figure of that group. Furthermore, once we ask questions of historical method concerning the use of rabbinical sayings and stories, we do well to study particular texts, specific problems. Hillel, then, provides both an important object of study in his own right, and also a significant example of how historical-critical issues must govern our study. In this chapter we pursue the analysis of the more important texts in various documents of the rabbinical canon, from the Mishnah through the two Talmuds, in which tales about Hillel or sayings attributed to Hillel appear.

Students therefore face the challenge of dealing with the actual texts of rabbinical writings. These texts are not so accessible to us as are their New Testament counterparts, stories about Jesus. They take up problems remote from our world—though close to the world of the biblical laws—and they approach those problems in ways in which, in general, we should not have predicted. Accordingly, it will require a measure of patience to work through remote and arcane discussions of issues no one really cares about anyhow. But to understand another world and its human issues, we have to listen patiently to alien minds and how they define and solve their problems. The translation should make the passages reasonably accessible, and the discussion of their literary and substantive characteristics then states what is relevant to our problem of historical inquiry.

HILLEL'S IMPORTANCE

Hillel's name predominates in the rabbinical traditions about the Pharisees. Indeed, the greater part of those traditions deals with him, the party of his followers, called the House of Hillel, and of their opponents within Pharisaism, Shammai and the House of Shammai.

Hillel was a near-contemporary of Jesus. The dates commonly assigned to him are ca. 50 B.C.E. to ca. 10 C.E. Some of his teachings, moreover, are in spirit and even in exact wording close to the teachings of Jesus. Such a well-known saying as the Golden Rule is attributed to Hillel in negative form: "What is hateful to yourself do not do to your neighbor. That is the entire Torah. All the rest is commentary. Now go forth and learn." That saying went from country to country and from culture to culture, always being attributed to the leading sage or wise man of the place. It is a virtually universal teaching of wisdom, and its attribution to Hillel tells us that he was regarded as the supreme authority within the Pharisaic movement.

Part of the reason for Hillel's predominance is that his followers took over the leadership of Pharisaic Judaism from the followers of Shammai. After 70 C.E. at Yavneh, on the coast of the Land of Israel, adherents of the House of Hillel were in charge of the formation of traditions about pre-70 times, just as they controlled the legal decisions of their own place and time.

HILLEL AS LEGISLATOR

Hillel is represented as a legislator who not only interpreted existing statutes, but made new and important changes in the law. His most important ordinance follows. The scriptural rule is that the advent of the Seventh Year in the septennial cycle carries with it remission of all debts. In consequence, people would not lend money to those in need, for fear they would not get it back. Hillel accommodated the law to the conditions of everyday life by creating a legal way out of the remission of debts by the Seventh Year. If the lender deposited a certificate, called the *prozbul*, in which the court took over the debts and preserved them from being annulled in the Seventh Year, then the debts would remain valid. Hence people could supply necessary small loans. The Scriptures refer to individuals ("Whatever of yours that is with your brother") but do not refer to property in the hands of the court ("Yours, not the court's").

A. *Whatever of yours that is with your brother your hand should release* (Deut. 15:3)—but not he who gives his mortgages to the court.

B. On this basis, they said

C. Hillel ordained the *prozbul*.

D. On account of the order of the world.

E. That he saw the people, that they held back from lending to one another and transgressed what is written in the Torah.

F. He arose and ordained the *prozbul*.

G. And this is the formula of the *prozbul*: "I give to you, so-and-so and so-and-so, the judges in such-and-such place, every debt which I have, that I may collect it whenever I like," and the judges seal below, or the witnesses (Sifré Deut. 113).

First comes the anonymous exegesis on which the *prozbul*, the document circumventing remission of debts in the Seventh Year, allegedly is based: debts in the hands of a court are not released by the advent of the sabbatical year. The rest of the pericope seems to depend upon the exegesis. In fact, parts C–D and E–F do not.

Part B suggests that Hillel ordained the *prozbul* on the basis of the scriptural exegesis, while part E gives another, different reason, not based upon scriptural exegesis at all, but upon a wordplay on *order/ordain* in verbal and nominative forms. Part C is a simple, stock phrase report of the whole matter. It could have stood with either part D or part B, but parts B and D make one another redundant.

The "historical event," part E, on which the *prozbul* is based poses a problem, for the same conditions that provoked the *prozbul* in Hillel's time surely pertained for many centuries. How can one explain why in *just* Hillel's time the people discovered the "evil impulse" described in Deut. 15:9–10? Part E actually is a "historical paraphrase" of Deut. 15:9–10:

Take heed lest there be a base thought in your heart and you say, "The Seventh Year, the year of release is near," and your eye be hostile to your poor brother and you give him nothing. . . . You shall give to him freely . . . because for this the Lord your God will bless you. . . . For the poor will never cease out of the land.

The absence of an explicit reference to this Scripture is striking (it *is* quoted in later versions), but the foregoing story about not lending before the year of release takes the place of the Scripture's description of this same "event." The story thus serves as an exegesis, through historical narrative, of Deut. 15:9–10.

Part F then repeats part C, adding the words *arose and* to supply a connection with part E, and thus to preserve the fictitious historical framework. Part G is tacked on; the story is complete without it. Part G could as well have followed part A. We do not know what Hillel said; part G ignores him, and part F satisfactorily completes his story. Including the formula is superfluous here, but makes good sense following part A. Presumably the anonymous exegesis consisted of part A + G, to which various Hillel materials are attached, first by assigning the exegesis to Hillel (parts B–C), then by making up a story (parts E–F).

Part B introduces the story: *On this basis*, referring to the exegesis, therefore tying the following to it, Hillel ordained the *prozbul*. The intrusion of *they said* makes no sense. We are not told *who* said. It is a stock introduction to a new story or clause. Actually it ties to the opening of part E, *they said that he saw*, or to part C, *they said that Hillel*. But part D and part E cannot be joined.

Two different stories therefore have been put together. One is parts A + B, C + G:

(But not he who gives)
On this basis (omit: *they said*)
Hillel ordained the *prozbul*
(And this is the formula)

The other is parts A + C, D, E, F + G:

(But not he who gives)
Hillel ordained
On account of the order of the world
(omit: *that*) He saw the people, that they held back
He arose and ordained

The version of parts A + B, C + G is the simplest statement of matters. Parts D, E, and F introduce a "historical" provocation for the matter, ignoring the exegesis and reporting an "event" to take its place. The two versions actually did circulate separately.

The viewpoint of the former version is that Hillel's action was based upon sound exegesis of Scripture, and did not represent modification of the law merely to accommodate the law to historical circumstances. Rather, the law always had been what Hillel now said, but it was Hillel who recognized that fact and acted upon it. Hillel's greatness is in recovering the tradition, not in inventing new laws to meet the needs of the time.

The contrary tendency ignores the exegesis. Hillel *did* change the law to accommodate it to the needs of the day. The decree was "for the order of the world" and had no exegetical basis in mosaic law. The specific problem that provoked changing the law therefore has to be spelled out. Others who choose to issue ordinances are similarly justified as circumstances require.

Not only did the two stories circulate separately, but the clumsy means by which they are amalgamated, for example, the repetition of the "reason" for the decree and the use of *that* both where it fits and where it does not fit, suggest that completed versions already existed before the pericope was put together.

We have no firm basis on which to formulate a theory of events. Perhaps Hillel actually made such a decree for the reasons specified, and the fact that he could do so underlines his immense power and prestige within Pharisaism. But that decree would not have affected the great numbers of Palestinian Jews who were not Pharisees. Debtors, moreover, were here given a good motive to dislike Pharisees, who now rendered their debts into a perpetual burden.

This leads to the possibility that the *prozbul* existed before Hillel's day. He served as a convenient name on which to hang Pharisaic acceptance of it, despite contravening scriptural law. But then the debtors' interest would become problematical. On one hand, the debts are now allowed to pile up and be carried forward. On the other hand, the theory of the *prozbul* for Pharisaic consumption is that it loosens credit. But both theories presuppose that the law was widely observed, and debts forgiven according to Deuteronomic law. Evidence of actual practice here becomes decisive; I know no evidence of what people actually did.

While historical considerations lead to an impasse, form-critical ones do not. The story represents the effort, first, to attribute the anonymous exegetical justification of the *prozbul* to Hillel, and then to combine both views of ordinances—a compromise between those who held that one may legislate to meet the needs of the day and those who held that legislation always depended upon scriptural exegesis. The latter believed exegesis was possible for all needed legislation. The former may have thought otherwise, or, more likely, had no sufficiently rich exegetical tradition that permitted them to rely upon scriptural exegesis for important matters.

It was Aqiba and his associates at Yavneh who so enriched the exegetical tradition of the rabbis that they could find whatever they wanted in Scripture. Earlier, before ca. 90 C.E., those who had to issue decrees without the Aqiban method thought it reasonable merely because the times obviously required it, for example, Yavneans from Yohanan b. Zakkai's time to Aqiba's. Their view of matters is consistently represented in stories of Yohanan's own decrees: Yohanan did what the times required, with or without scriptural proof. It was natural to shape Hillelite materials in the same framework, even where it distorted the materials. It seems likely that the first viewpoint would appropriately derive from circles influenced by Aqiban exegetical innovations, the second from circles in which those innovations were either unknown or unacceptable. The second might be the older of the two, but it is no more credible, from a historical viewpoint, on that account.

HILLEL'S WISE SAYINGS

To Hillel are attributed numerous wise sayings, many more than to all other Pharisaic masters put together. The most famous is the Golden Rule. Others are as follows:

Hillel says, "Be of the disciples of Aaron, loving peace, and pursuing peace, loving mankind, and bringing them near to the Torah."

He used to say, "A name made great is a name destroyed, and he that increases not decreases, and he that learns not is worthy of death, and he that makes worldly use of the crown perishes."

He used to say, "If I am not for myself who is for me? and being for mine own self, what am I? And if not now, when?" (M. Avot 1:12–14).

With flaming fire at his right hand (Deut. 33:3):

Just as fire makes a mark on the flesh of whoever touches it, so whoever makes profit in matters of Torah loses his life.

For so would Hillel say, "*And he who uses the crown shall perish . . .*" (Midrash Tannaim, ed. David Hoffmann, 211).

A. Hillel said, "(1) Do not separate from the congregation; and (2) do not trust yourself until the day of your death; and (3) do not judge your fellow until you come to his place; and (4) do not say a thing which cannot be heard, for it will be heard in the end; and (5) say not, 'When I have leisure I will study.' Perhaps you will not have leisure."

B. He used to say, "(6) A brutish man dreads not sin; and (7) an ignorant man cannot be saintly; and (8) the bashful man cannot learn; and (9) the impatient man cannot teach; and (10) he that engages overmuch in trade cannot become wise; and (11) where there are no men, strive to be a man."

C. Also he once saw one skull floating on the face of the water. He said to it, (12) "*Because you drowned others, they drowned you, and at the last they that drowned you shall be drowned.*"

D. He used to say, (13) "The more [=He who multiplies] flesh, the more worms; (14) the more possessions, the more care; (15) the more women, the more witchcraft; (16) the more slave women, the more thieving; (17) the more Torah, the more life; (18) the more schooling, the more wisdom; (19) the more counsel, the more understanding; (20) the more righteousness, the more peace. (21) If a man has gained a good name he has gained [it] for himself; (22) if he has gained for himself words of Torah, he has gained for himself life in the world to come" (M. Avot 2:5-7).

The italicized logia are in Aramaic, the rest in Hebrew. The pericope is a collection of moral sayings, in the simplest structure. The various clauses are joined by *and, he used to say,* or, in the case of part C, *also.* A "historical" narrative setting is invented for the saying about the skull.

The twenty-three separate sayings are not all of the same kind. The first five are separate, unrelated logia, with *and* merely a connecting word; where the thematic connection is obvious, as in the antonymic parts later on, no *and* is supplied. Part B contains five related, evenly balanced sayings, and then an independent logion (no. 11). Part C, as noted, is a separate logion which is given a narrative setting. Part D returns to the model of part B, in which 13–16 are balanced pairs of negative characteristics, 17–20 positive ones, as follows:

flesh/worms	Torah/life
possessions/care	schooling/wisdom
women/witchcraft	counsel/understanding
women/lewdness	righteousness/peace
slave women/thieving	

Then come 21 and 22, the contrast between the good name for oneself and the words of Torah for life in the world to come.

It is difficult to imagine parts D and B as composites of separate sayings. They are clearly arranged to make a single point through a set of discrete examples. Part C is a separate *narrative + logion,* and part A is a composite of logia. The likelihood is that once the form had been stated, it generated many new examples.

That such sayings circulated in Hillel's name before 200 C.E. is unlikely, since none is ever quoted, referred to, or attributed to him prior to the third-century masters. This is prima facie evidence that the whole is late. But other such balanced syzygies of moral sayings occur in Hillel's name, perhaps accounting for the attribution to him of any that followed the same pattern, or generating new sayings according to the original formula.

The preceding pericope obviously is a composite. Parts B, C, and D represent substantial developments into rather sophisticated forms—the first and the last are balanced images, the middle a story.

None can be regarded as primitive. The sayings in part **A**, famous in their own right, presumably were popular proverbs assigned to Hillel.

> A. R. Sadoq says, "Keep not aloof from the congregation, and do not make yourself like those who seek to influence the judges. Make them [words of Torah] not a crown wherewith to magnify yourself or a spade wherewith to dig."
>
> B. And thus Hillel used to say, "*He that makes worldly use of the crown shall perish.*"
>
> C. Thus you may learn that he that makes profit out of words of Torah takes his life from the world (M. Avot 4:5).

Hillel's *worldly use* saying now serves as a gloss on the saying of Sadoq, a later master in Jerusalem and early Yavneh. It circulated as an independent logion. The italicized words are in Aramaic. The Hebrew subscription (part C) supplies a commentary.

Citation of Hillel's saying as a gloss on Sadoq's proves nothing about the antiquity of the former. An editor, shaping the whole, might well have drawn the Hillel saying from available materials. Sadoq need not have heard it. If he had, he presumably would have cited it, or alluded to its striking image, in the name of Hillel. He refers to a crown; hence the editor brought together two *crown* sayings originally circulating independently of one another.

> Hillel the Elder says:
>
> 1. "Do not be seen naked; do not be seen clothed.
>
> 2. "Do not be seen standing; and do not be seen sitting.
>
> 3. "Do not be seen laughing, and do not be seen weeping, for it is said, *There is a time to laugh and a time to weep, a time to embrace and a time to refrain from embracing* (Qoh. 3:4–5)" (Tos. Ber. 2:21).
>
> Hillel the Elder says:
>
> 4. "When they are gathering, scatter, and when they are scattering, gather.
>
> 5. "When you see that the Torah is beloved of all Israel and all rejoice in it, you scatter it abroad, as it is said, *Some scatter and gain more* (Prov. 11:24).
>
> 6. "When you see the Torah is forgotten in Israel and not everyone pays attention to it, you gather it in, as it is said, *A time to work for the Lord* (Ps. 119:126)" (Tos. Ber. 6:24).

Tos. Ber. 2:21 is a set of matched amplifications of the teaching not to separate oneself from the community. One should not do what the community at large is not doing, and vice versa, one should not refrain from doing what the community at large is doing. But study of Torah is an exception.

The meaning of Tos. Ber. 6:24 is that when the disciples come together to appreciate and review teachings of Torah, they should "scatter," that is, teach widely. But when teachings are lost and people forget the Torah, then they should engage in independent study, without trying to educate the masses. The saying thus applies the foregoing rules to study of Torah: One should not do the opposite of what the community is doing, but, in regard to Torah, one cannot waste Torah traditions on a heedless audience or stop his own study because others are not interested. So the two sayings form a coherent, antonymic pair. But they do not circulate as a pair, and are never brought into relationship.

Both sets of logia obviously are highly developed, indeed are even supplied with appropriate proof texts. The three examples of Tos. Ber. 2:21 are matched by the three of Tos. Ber. 6:24, though any one of the three might have stood by itself and made its own point. I do not think we are dealing with six independent logia, but rather with two sets.

THE LEGEND OF HILLEL'S
RISE TO POWER

The most complex set of Hillel traditions deals with his rise to power. He came from Babylonia as an obscure immigrant, but, miraculously, his learning was recognized, and he was made *Nasi*, or patriarch. We shall consider part of the repertoire of versions of this story, first the Tosefta's, then the Palestinian Talmud's, noting how the first and simple example is later embellished according to various tendencies. For in order of redaction, the Tosefta is earliest, the Palestinian Talmud second, the Babylonian Talmud third. The third is omitted for the present purpose.

A. One time the fourteenth [of Nisan, the eve of Passover] fell on the Sabbath.

They asked Hillel the Elder, "Does the *Pesah* [Passover offering] override the Sabbath? [That is, is the Passover sacrifice offered on the Sabbath?]"

He said to them, "And do we have only one *Pesah* in the year which overrides the Sabbath? We have many more than three hundred *Pesahs* in the year, and they override the Sabbath."

The meaning is that many sacrifices override the Sabbath. How so? During the year hundreds of sacrifices are offered on that day, including the two daily burnt offerings and the two additional sacrifices of every Sabbath, besides extra sacrifices offered on the Sabbath that occurs in the middle of the week of Passover and the week of Tabernacles. Hillel, however, dissimulates, for the question is not, Does one make a sacrifice on the Sabbath? Everyone knows one does so. The issue is, Do we make this particular offering, in connection with the Passover, on that day? When Hillel replies that "many *Pesahs* override the Sabbath," he thus says the Passover offering is no different from the normal cultic offerings carried out through the year.

> B. The whole courtyard collected against him.
> He said to them, "The continual offering is a community sacrifice, and the *Pesah* is a community sacrifice. Just as the continual offering, a community sacrifice, overrides the Sabbath, so the *Pesah* is a community sacrifice and overrides the Sabbath.

This reply is more to the point, for now Hillel explicitly states that he regards the Passover sacrifice as no different from the continual offering. The two have in common the fact that the community is responsible for supplying them. Hence they will have in common other traits as well.

> C. "Another matter: It is said concerning the continual offering: *In its season* (Num. 28:2), and it is said with reference to the *Pesah*:
> *In its season* (Num. 9:2). Just as the continual offering, concerning which *In its season* is said, overrides the Sabbath, so the *Pesah*, concerning which *In its season* is said, overrides the Sabbath."

The comparison to the continual offering is developed, now in relationship to Scriptures. Scriptures use the same language with reference to both the Passover offering and the continual offering. This shows the two are comparable and will be subject to the same rules.

> D. "And furthermore [it is a] *qal vehomer* [argument a fortiori]: Although the continual offering, which does not produce the [severe] liability of *cutting off*, overrides the Sabbath, the *Pesah*, which *does* produce the liability of *cutting off*—is it not logical that it should override the Sabbath?
> E. "And further, I have received from my masters [the tradition] that the *Pesah* overrides the Sabbath, and not [merely] the first *Pesah* but the second, and not [merely] the community *Pesah* but the individual *Pesah* [as well]."

Hillel now claims that the foregoing arguments do not matter, for he has a tradition from his masters, who are not specified, that the Passover sacrifice is to be offered on the Sabbath. The question then arises, if so, what should people do who, not knowing the law, did not make proper preparations to make the offering?

> F. They said to him, "What will be the rule for the people who on the Sabbath did not bring knives and *Pesah* offerings to the sanctuary?"
> G. He said to them, "Leave them alone. The holy spirit is upon them. If they are not prophets, they are disciples of the prophets."
> H. What did Israel [the Jews] do in that hour? He whose *Pesah* was a lamb hid it in its wool; if it was a kid, he tied it between its horns; so they brought knives and *Pesahs* to the sanctuary and slew the *Pesah* sacrifices.
> I. On that very day they appointed Hillel as *Nasi*, and he would teach to them concerning the laws of the *Pesah* (Tos. Pisha 4:13).

The pericope is transparently composite, a collection of loosely related traditions on Hillel's dispute with "them," and his consequent elevation to the position of *Nasi*. The dispute supplies a dramatic, narrative setting for exegeses which could have stood separately, anonymously, and without such a setting. The stories of Hillel's rise to power thus were joined with exegeses of *Pesah* and the Sabbath.

Part A introduces the whole matter and is complete in itself: Hillel was asked and thereupon supplied a complete and final answer. The following arguments are attached to it by the *whole courtyard* supposedly disagreeing with him, but saying nothing in response to his repertoire. Later on "they" would be named, still later "they" would demolish his arguments.

The arguments are as follows:

> A. Many *Pesahs* override the Sabbath;
> B. Community sacrifices such as the Passover offering override the Sabbath;
> C. *Its season* applies both to continual offering and to *Pesah*, thus both override Sabbath;
> D. *Qal vehomer* [argument a fortiori];
> E. I have a *tradition* from my masters.

Nothing is said about who the masters are. This would be added later on.

In part F the response is given: Everyone forthwith agrees. Part F could as well have followed part A (or any of the subsequent arguments), but is held back until the whole repertoire is completed.

Part G is a still further, separate element, in which a probably well-known apothegm ("If they are not prophets . . .") is attributed to Hillel, followed by part H, an illustration of the prophetic heritage. The people can be relied on, because they do have access to the holy spirit, or at least automatically do the right thing.

Then comes part I, *on that very day*. The House of Hillel persistently appealed to the holy spirit and other supernatural informants in deciding questions of law. But no claim of supernatural revelation was asserted in Hillel's behalf. On the contrary, his failure to receive the holy spirit had to be explained away.

Distinguishing the exegetical from the narrative elements, we find the following:

Narrative	Exegetical
A. One time	A. Many *Pesahs* override
B. Joined issue [or E.]	B. Community sacrifices
F. What to do?	C. *In its season*
G. Holy spirit	D. *Qal vehomer*
H. What did people do?	E. Tradition
I. They made him *Nasi*	

We see, therefore, that except for A or E, but not both, the exegetical and dispute materials are independent of the narrative framework; all, including A and E, are inserted without much, if any, reference to the narrative details. We can reconstruct the event without referring to the exegetical argumentation. The composite pericope gives every evidence of coming at the end of a long process of development. The problem of the *Pesah* comes before the arguments. The story of the rise to power is developed in its own terms. Then the two are combined.

As to the historical framework, we are told that for generations no one had known what to do when the eve of Passover, the fourteenth of Nisan, fell on the Sabbath, until Hillel came along and told them. Yet this contradicts part E and parts G–H, in which we are told, "You *can* rely on what the people normally do and do not have to depend upon exegetical investigation, except for ex post facto justification for accepted practice." Later on this anomaly is explained, with reference to part E.

This state of affairs is tied to the foregoing by the explanation that Hillel himself had approved referring to popular practice, saying that the people are under the holy spirit. Since other sayings concerning Hillel allege that he alone of his generation was worthy of receiving the holy spirit, but the generation in which he lived was of such poor character that the holy spirit was withheld in their day even from Hillel, the pericope must be set apart from other sorts of Hillel traditions. But I cannot suggest who would have wanted to allege in Hillel's name that the holy spirit is upon Israel, or what polemic was involved in so stating.

Part A contradicts parts F–G, for part A alleges no one knew what to do until Hillel came, and parts F–G claim everyone knew precisely what to do, but Hillel was able either to provide adequate exegetical authority or to cite masters. But no one else in Jerusalem had heard anything from those same masters on this subject.

Shemaiah and Abtalion, supposedly his teachers, are not mentioned, probably because at the outset it would have been incredible that only Hillel knew their teaching about a matter of Temple procedure that must have arisen several times in their lifetimes alone. But later they are inserted as a gloss on "my masters." The anomaly then has to be explained: "You were too lazy to study with Shemaiah and Abtalion. That is why you did not know their traditions."

The little narrative in part H is a separate story, without any real connection to the rest except *in that hour*, which, like *one time* and *on that very day*, is a convenient joining formula for the historical-narrative framework. These considerations require further division of the narrative framework into part A and parts F, G, and H; part I is still a third element in the narrative.

The anonymity of the pericope, the clumsy joining of its composite elements into a single, unitary account, and the historical dubiety of the story that Hillel's arguments were accepted by Temple authorities and he was therefore made patriarch or *Nasi* over the Temple all point to a relatively late date for the story as a whole. I do not see how anyone could have made it up or put it together while the Temple was standing, for at that point no one could have believed it. My guess is that available exegetical elements were claimed for Hillel after the narrative parts were put together; then Hillel's name could be supplied for *any* exegesis proving that the *Pesah* offering overrides the Sabbath. The arguments could have been worked out at the same period, then attached to the story of Hillel's rise to power, once the issue of the *Pesah* was established as the primary theme of that story.

The obvious division in the narrative is between the elements that say Hillel became *Nasi* because of the excellence of his exegetical ingenuity, and those that say he became *Nasi* because he had a tradition from his masters. But here that distinction does not seem to be important. In the Palestinian and Babylonian talmudic versions, it is developed into a major polemic. No one dramatically underlines that Hillel was ignored until he could quote his masters, for part E is pretty much equivalent to the foregoing. Hence the real contrast is between the allegation that people do know what to do and do not require rabbinical instruction, but merely rabbinical confirmation for what they already do, and the thesis that until Hillel's exegeses, no one, even his masters, knew what to do at all. I am not sure who would have wanted to advance the former theory, but since it seems to me to claim less for Hillel, I imagine it would not have come from the patriarchal circles, who would have preferred the view that Hillel was superior even to his masters, Shemaiah and Abtalion. It seems unlikely to me that any of this contains a shred of historically usable information.

The next version, which occurs in the Palestinian Talmud, first introduces the names of Hillel's opposition. They now are the "Elders of Bathyra." The Bathyrans were Babylonian Jewish immigrants who came at the time of Herod and were settled in frontier regions, northeast of the Sea of Galilee, to protect the border. They founded the town of Bathyra, whence the name. Herod put some of them into the Temple hierarchy. They next turn up at Yavneh, where they are represented as opposing Yohanan b. Zakkai's right to make liturgical decisions formerly vested in the Temple. At the end of the second century, Judah the Patriarch alludes to the Bathyrans giving up their office to his ancestor Hillel. This means that the story which we are about to consider was known, in substantially its present form, by Judah's time. The version just considered, which ignores the Bathyrans, has to come well before Judah the Patriarch. Numerous other glosses embellish the earlier account; the elements of Tos. Pisha are rearranged in various ways.

A. This law was lost to the Elders of Bathyra.

B. One time the fourteenth [of Nisan] turned out to coincide with the Sabbath, and they did not know whether the *Pesah* [Passover offering] overrides the Sabbath or not.

They said, "There is here a certain Babylonian, and Hillel is his name, who studied with Shemaiah and Abtalion. [He] knows whether the *Pesah* overrides the Sabbath or not. Perhaps there will be profit from him."

They sent and called him.

C. They said to him, "Have you ever heard, when the fourteenth [of Nisan] coincides with the Sabbath, whether it overrides the Sabbath or not?"

D. He said to them, "And do we have only one *Pesah* alone that overrides the Sabbath in the whole year? And do not many *Pesahs* override the Sabbath in the whole year?"

E. (Some Tannaim teach a hundred, and some Tannaim teach two hundred, and some Tannaim teach three hundred.

He who said one hundred [refers to] continual offerings.

He who said two hundred [refers to] continual offerings and Sabbath additional offerings.

He who said three hundred [refers to] continual offerings, Sabbath additional offerings, [and those] of festivals, and of New Moons, and of seasons.)

E. They said to him, "We have already said that there is with you profit."

F. He began expounding for them by means of arguments based on *heqqesh, qal vehomer,* and *gezerah shavah:*

G. "*Heqqesh:* Since the continual offering is a community sacrifice and the *Pesah* is a community sacrifice, just as the continual offering, a community sacrifice, overrides [the] Sabbath, so the *Pesah*, a community sacrifice, overrides the Sabbath.

H. "*Qal vehomer:* If the continual offering, [improperly] doing which does not produce the liability of cutting off, overrides the Sabbath, the *Pesah*, [improperly] doing which *does* produce the liability of cutting off, all the more so should override the Sabbath.

I. "*Gezerah shavah:* Concerning the continual offering, *In its season* is said (Num. 28:2), and concerning the *Pesah, In its season* is said (Num. 9:3). Just as the continual offering, concerning which is said *In its season* overrides the Sabbath, so the *Pesah*, concerning which *In its season* is said, overrides the Sabbath."

J. They said to him, "We have already said, 'There is no profit [benefit] from the Babylonian.'"

K. "As to the *heqqesh* which you said, there is a reply: No—for if you say so concerning the continual offering, there is a limit to the continual offering, but can you say so concerning the *Pesah*, which has no limit?" [The two are different, and the same rule therefore cannot apply.]

L. "The *qal vehomer* which you stated has a reply: No—if you say so concerning the continual offering, which is the most sacred, will you say so of the *Pesah*, which is of lesser sanctity?" [So the argument collapses.]

M. "As to the *gezerah shavah* that you said: A man may not reason a *gezerah shavah* on his own [but must cite it from tradition]. . . ."

N. Even though he sat and expounded for them all day, they did not accept [it] from him, until he said to them, "May [evil] come upon me! Thus have I heard from Shemaiah and Abtalion!"

When they heard this from him, they arose and appointed him *Nasi* over them.

O. When they had appointed him *Nasi* over them, he began to criticize them, saying, "Who caused you to need this Babylonian? Is it not because you did not serve the two great men of the world, Shemaiah and Abtalion, who were sitting with you?"

P. Since he criticized them, the law was forgotten by him.

Q. They said to him, "What shall we do for the people who did not bring their knives?"

R. He said to them, "This law have I heard, but I have forgotten [it]. But leave Israel [alone]. If they are not prophets, they are disciples of prophets."

S. Forthwith, whoever had a lamb as his *Pesah* would hide it [knife] in its wool; [if] it was a kid he would tie the knife between its horns. So their *Pesahs* turned out to be bringing their knives with them.

T. When he saw the deed, he remembered the law.

U. He said, "Thus have I heard from Shemaiah and Abtalion" (Palestinian Talmud Pesahim 6:1).

The pericope before us is a veritable repertoire of traditions on Hillel and the Temple—but apart from the superscription, part A, the Bathyrans are completely forgotten. That detail must have been added last. Linking Hillel to the fall of the Bathyrans certainly comes after the formation, around Hillel's discipleship of Shemaiah and Abtalion, of the bulk of the materials on his rise to power. The essential story is contained in the following parts:

B. No one knew what to do when Passover, the fourteenth of Nisan, coincided with the Sabbath, so "a certain Babylonian" is called, because of his discipleship of Shemaiah and Abtalion.

C. He is asked the question.

D. He says the answer is obvious: Many *pesahs* override the Sabbath!

E. They accept his explanation.

At this point, the story could have ended; nothing is required to complete the picture. We do not have to be told about the immediate abdiction (N) of the Bathyrans. That "event" is no issue.

Part E is certainly a late gloss on part D; Tos. Pisha has already corrected the language of *many* to read *three hundred*, which I assume is a scribal improvement of an otherwise older version.

Then comes a new and different repertoire of materials: Hillel's proofs. We have no reason to attribute them to Hillel himself. They are additional "proofs" anyone might have supplied for the same proposition, an exercise in exegetical logic independent of the historical setting:

   F. Superscription for the whole.
   G. *Heqqesh.*
   H. *Qal vehomer.*
   I. *Gezerah shavah.*
   K. Refutation of *heqqesh.*
   L. Refutation of *qal vehomer.*
   M. Refutation of *gezerah shavah.*

After part I comes a revision of part E, this time in negative form. Having accepted his proof, "they" now reject it! Part J certainly marks the end of a separate and complete version. Parts K, L, and M explain the rejection of proofs attributed to Hillel.

Part N is a separate element in the story, joined to the foregoing by "even though he sat and expounded." The point is that he has a tradition from his teachers, Shemaiah and Abtalion, on which basis he is made *Nasi.* This now concludes Hillel's proofs and artificially links them to the "historical" account.

Afterward comes another, separate story concerning Hillel's gloating at the fall of the Bathyrans. It underlines the importance of serving Shemaiah and Abtalion, and in fact represents a secondary development of part N: Hillel came to office only because he had studied with Shemaiah and Abtalion; the Bathyrans lost office only because they had not paid them adequate attention.

Part P is a connecting element, leading into a third story referring to what to do for the people who had not brought their knives. Obviously, Hillel knew the answer—that is the point of the foregoing. But since the narrator intends to tell how the people are really prophets, he makes Hillel forget what he had learned, because of a moral lapse! This allows the famous logion to be stated by Hillel: "Leave Israel alone. If they are not prophets. . . ." The saying is then illustrated by the behavior of the people. The theme of part P is recovered in parts T-U ("he remembered the law"). Then comes the phrase: *Thus have I heard.* . . .

The foregoing analysis leads to division of the whole pericope into the following separate parts:

1. Parts B, C, D, E: Hillel solves the problem, all agree.
2. Parts F–M + N: Repertoire of exegetical proofs, all refuted. Part N may have been contributed by the final editorial hand, tying the whole to part A—but in doing so, the editor has repeated part U.
3. Parts O-P: Hillel underlines the fault of the opposition, but is supernaturally punished on that account.

4. Parts Q–S, with subscription T–U: The people knew what to do all along, because they are disciples of prophets. Hillel thereupon says their practice conformed to the law.

Let us now reconsider the picture presented by each of the four elements.

1. B, C, D, E: No one knew the law. Hillel, who had studied with Shemaiah and Abtalion, was listened to on that account. He said the answer was obvious, and others forthwith agreed.

The tendency of the first story is to stress that Hillel knew the law, *but* was recognized only because of his discipleship of Shemaiah and Abtalion. However, as soon as he stated the law, *without* referring to and quoting his masters, everyone exclaimed in agreement.

2. F, G, H, I, J, K, L, M, N: Hillel tried every logical-exegetical device, without success. Finally he said the tradition comes from Shemaiah-Abtalion, and the opposition thereupon abdicated and made him *Nasi*.

The tendency of the first story is underlined. Now Hillel's knowledge is of no consequence; all that matters is the ability to cite Shemaiah and Abtalion. But once he could do so, the opposition not merely agrees, but abdicates office and places Hillel in it instead! So Hillel owes his power to his discipleship, not to his logic. Discipleship is the key to authority, while mere ability to reason makes no difference.

3. O–P: When Hillel became *Nasi*, he behaved so obnoxiously that heaven punished him by depriving him of what had made him *Nasi* to begin with: knowledge of the traditions of Shemaiah and Abtalion.

The story follows the same tendency as the foregoing.

4. Q, R, S, T, U: Hillel did not know the law. He observed what people did and was reminded that the people were following the correct procedures as enunciated by Shemaiah and Abtalion.

The four stories make much the same point through the reworking of various materials. Hillel's importance depends upon Shemaiah and Abtalion. Without knowing *their* traditions, he would not have been recognized and would not have persuaded the opposition.

The redactor of the stories stands outside of the Hillelite circle and, of course, comes well after its predominance was an established fact. Everyone knows who "the certain Babylonian" is, and is well aware of his rise to power.

The real question is, why did the redactor of the whole, as well as those responsible for the formation of the several parts, choose to emphasize Hillel's utter subordination to his masters, a theme virtually absent in the earlier version? Whatever the brilliance of one's logic, possessing accurate traditions from a recognized master is decisive. Who would have wanted to say so, and to whom? No story about Hillel in power can have failed to reflect the importance of the later patriarchate, and the importance to the patriarchate, from ca. 150 C.E. onward, of Hillel stories.

Is a patriarchal interest at hand? I do not see any. The patriarch would not necessarily have objected to all elements of the portrayal of Hillel; his rise to power is represented as creditable.

But an obvious antipatriarchal tendency appears in division 3, and somewhat more subtly in division 4: the *Nasi* may be punished by Heaven for harassing the rest of the sages. Hillel was no better than others. Since everyone knew what he knew, all he could contribute was the attribution to Shemaiah and Abtalion. Divisions 1–2 consistently portray Hillel as important because of his masters, but we need not hear an echo that the *Nasi* had better listen to his masters, since no one openly accused the *Nasi* of "ignorance." So the story has been developed into a polemic in favor of discipleship. The patriarch thus is warned that the collegium of the rabbinical masters is decisive in the formation of the law.

HILLEL AND SHAMMAI

In the beginning were the House of Shammai and the House of Hillel, presumably dating from ca. 10 C.E. to 70 C.E. Afterward came the traditions about Shammai and Hillel themselves. That is to say, the earliest well-attested traditions about pre-70 times, emanating from the academy of Yavneh after 70, deal with the legal traditions attributed to these two groups within Pharisaism. Only much later, after the Bar Kokba War, do we find attestations for stories about the founders of the Houses.

The relationship between the Houses of Shammai and Hillel thus produced stories about the relationship between the founding fathers, Shammai and Hillel. While the materials concerning the houses are fair and balanced, and give equal respect to the opinions of each side, the stories about the founding fathers do not. On the contrary, the Hillelites, responsible for the entire corpus of Hillel-Shammai stories, consistently represent Shammai unfavorably. One example of this tendency follows:

A. Our rabbis taught:

A man should always be gentle like Hillel, and not impatient like Shammai.

B. It once happened that two men made a wager with each other, saying "He who goes and makes Hillel angry shall receive four hundred zuz."

Said one, "I will anger him."

That day was the Sabbath eve, and Hillel was washing his head. He went, passed by the door of his house, and called out, "Is Hillel here? Is Hillel here?"

Thereupon he robed and went out him, saying, "My son, what do you seek?"

"I have a question to ask," said he.

"Ask, my son," he said to him.

He asked, "Why are heads of the Babylonians round?"

"My son, you have asked a great question," he said. "Because they have no skillful midwives."

He departed, tarried a while, returned, and said, "Is Hillel here? Is Hillel here?"

He robed and went out to him, saying, "My son, what do you seek?"

"I have a question to ask," said he.

"Ask, my son," he said.

He asked, "Why are the eyes of the Palmyreans bleared?"

"My son, you have asked a great question," said he. "Because they live in sandy places."

He departed, tarried a while, returned, and said, "Is Hillel here? Is Hillel here?"

He robed and went out to him, saying, "My son, what do you seek?"

"I have a question to ask," said he. "Ask, my son," he said.

He asked, "Why are the feet of the Africans wide?"

"My son, you have asked a great question," said he. "Because they live in watery marshes."

"I have many questions to ask," said he, "but fear that you may become angry."

Thereupon he robed, sat before him, and said, "Ask all the questions you have to ask."

"Are you the Hillel whom they call the Nasi of Israel?"

"Yes," he said.

"If that is you," he said, "may there not be many like you in Israel."

"Why, my son?" said he.

"Because I have lost four hundred zuz through you," complained he.

"Be careful of your moods," he answered.

"Hillel is worth it that you should lose four hundred zuz and yet another four hundred zuz through him, yet Hillel shall not lose his temper."

C. Our rabbis taught:

A certain heathen once came before Shammai and asked him, "How many Torahs have you?"

"Two," he replied, "The Written Torah and the Oral Torah."

"I believe you with respect to the Written Torah, but not with respect to the Oral Torah. Make me a proselyte on condition that you teach me the Written Torah [only]."

He scolded and repulsed him in anger.

[When] he went before Hillel, he accepted him as a proselyte.

On the first day he taught him, *alef, bet, gimmel, delet* [=A, B, C, D]; the following day he reversed [them] to him.

"But yesterday you did not teach them to me thus," he said.

"Must you not rely upon me? Then rely upon me with respect to the Oral [Torah] too."

D. On another occasion it happened that a certain heathen came before Shammai and said to him, "Make me a proselyte, on condition that you teach me the whole Torah while I stand on one foot."

Thereupon he repulsed him with the builder's cubit which was in his hand.

[When] he went before Hillel, he converted him.

He said to him, "What is hateful to you, do not to your neighbor. That is the whole Torah, while the rest is the commentary thereof; go and learn [it]."

E. On another occasion it happened that a certain heathen was passing behind a school and heard the voice of a scribe reciting, "And these are the garments which they shall make: a breastplate, and an ephod."

Said he, "For whom are these?"

"For the High Priest," they said.

Then said that heathen to himself, "I will go and become a proselyte, that I may be appointed to a High Priest."

So he went before Shammai and said to him, "Make me a proselyte on condition that you appoint me a High Priest."

But he repulsed him with the builder's cubit which was in his hand.

He then went before Hillel. He made him a proselyte.

Said he to him, "Can any man be made a king but he who knows the arts of government? Go and study the arts of government!"

He went and read. When he came to *And the stranger that cometh nigh shall be put to death*, he asked him, "To whom does this verse apply?"

"Even to David, King of Israel," was the answer.

Thereupon that proselyte reasoned within himself a fortiori [*qal behomer*]: "If Israel, who are called sons of the Omnipresent, and whom in His love for them He designated *Israel is my son, my first born* (Exod. 4:22), yet it is written of them, *And the stranger that cometh nigh shall be put to death*—how much more so a mere proselyte, who comes with his staff and wallet!"

Then he went before Shammai and said to him, "Am I then eligible to be a High Priest? Is it not written in the Torah, *And the stranger that cometh nigh shall be put to death?*"

He went before Hillel and said to him, "O gentle Hillel: blessings rest on your head for bringing me under the wings of the *Shekhinah* [divine Presence]!"

F. Some time later the three met in one place. Said they, "Shammai's impatience sought to drive us from the world, but Hillel's gentleness brought us under the wings of the *Shekhinah*" (Babylonian Talmud Sabbat 30b–31a).

We have four separate stories, united with a superscription (part A) and subscription (part E). The stories as a group are in graceful Hebrew style. They certainly could have been told separately, but have been collected to make a single point, given at the end: Hillel was patient, Shammai querulous. The editor of the whole pericope has carefully supplied the moral of the stories.

Part C could have ended with the phrase noting that Hillel made him a proselyte, the intention of which is repeated in parts D and E. The alphabet story is a separate element, but relates closely to the preceding story. Parts D and E likewise seem to be unitary accounts from a single hand. Part F reverts to the superscription, now spelling out what the patience of Hillel had meant.

The four stories of course reflect the Hillelite viewpoint, but we have no idea which Hillelites—early or late, patriarchal or rabbinical, Palestinian or Babylonian. I discern only a few stock phrases, such as "Hillel is worth," "Be gentle like Hillel *and* not impatient like Shammai." But extended, detailed, smooth stories such as these are not built upon such brief stock phrases; they merely draw upon them at critical turning points or climaxes in the original narrative. Another well-known saying is the Aramaic *What is hateful . . . ,* around which the second act of part D is built.

THE HISTORICAL HILLEL

Our analysis of stories about Hillel repeatedly brings us to the rabbinical academies and patriarchal politics of the period after 70 C.E. When we are able to locate a master who knows a Hillel story, and who may therefore supply us with a date as to the *terminus a quo* of such a story, he usually is an authority after the Bar Kokba War, ca. 140 C.E., or even later. So we may claim that it is after 140 that Hillel as an individual, apart from the House that bears his name, becomes a central figure. His migration from Babylonia is taken for granted, and his rise to power is the subject of serious historical efforts. Some of his moral sayings and ordinances are first attested to then. There was interest in recovering usable spiritual heroes from within Pharisaism itself, in place of Bar Kokba and other messianic types.

The immense corpus of Hillel traditions exhibits one uniform quality: Unlike stories about Shammai, which are rarely friendly, no story is overtly hostile to Hillel. None was shaped by circles intending an unfavorable account of the man and his teachings. This is because the traditions were shaped by Hillelite heirs, both those who claimed to be his disciples, such as Yohanan b. Zakkai, and those, such as Gamaliel II, Simeon b. Gamaliel II, the House of Hillel, and especially Judah the Patriarch, who claimed to be his descendants. Indeed, the whole corpus of mishnaic literature was shaped by Hillelites.

Hillel pericopes served to supply points of origin for many legal and literary phenomena. Stories about Hillel as a model for virtue stand pretty much by themselves. Later masters made extensive use of the name of Hillel. From the destruction of the Temple onward, Hillel was everywhere claimed as the major authority—after Moses and Ezra—for the Oral Torah. Hillel could always be added to make stories more impressive. There was no limit to the claims made in his behalf as source of Torah traditions.

Despite the rich and impressive Hillel tradition, however, we can hardly conclude that with Hillel the rabbinic traditions about pre-70 C.E. Pharisees enter the pages of history. The traditions concerning Hillel do not lay a considerable claim to historical plausibility. They provide an accurate account only of what later generations thought important to say about, or in the name of, Hillel.

After 70 C.E. traditions about a man were shaped by his immediate disciples and discussed by people who actually knew him. Remarks about these traditions, made out of context in other settings, frequently provide attestation that a living tradition of what a master had said and done was shaped very soon after his death, and even during his lifetime. They often supply a *terminus a quo*. That does not mean the master actually said and did what the disciples and later contemporaries claim, but it does mean we stand close to the master. Reduction of the sayings and traditions to formal logia, even to written notes, and later to published compilations (such as the Mishnah) further contributes to the historical interest of the later masters' traditions.

Hillel's materials, by contrast, do not exhibit the marks of similar, exact processes of nearly contemporary editing and redaction, whether to oral form or to written documents. To Hillel are assigned neither masters nor disciples. He does not quote anyone, except in the context of a historical narrative, and then he does not repeat what "they" said to him, merely reports their law. No master of his day or before the Yavnean period ever quotes or even knows about him. He is supposed to have been the leading master of his time, but no one ever says, "So have I received from Hillel."

On the face of it, therefore, both form and style of the Hillel corpus differ from later materials. If Hillel is the first Pharisee to emerge in the model of the later first-century Pharisees and later rabbis, it is because the later rabbis adopted him and made him their own, not because he managed to transmit his sayings. The rabbis adopted him because of the later patriarchal claim to descend from him. It became interesting to tell stories about Hillel. Those who favored the patriarch would emphasize Hillel's merits; those who criticized the patriarch might stress that Hillel's virtue lay in his knowledge of Torah, not in his political role. Similarly, the House of Hillel's advocates in Yavneh and Usha had a strong motive to develop stories about the founder of their House. So the growth of the Hillel tradition was fostered by several distinct groups, and through their stories the several groups were able to address themselves to their own issues.

For the moment all we can say with certainty is that successive groups found it important to shape Hillel materials, and the conditions reflected in these materials are often not actual historical realities (no Pharisee, even Hillel, ran the Temple), but rather are the realities of life and fantasies of the shapers of the pericopes. The historical Hillel may stand behind some of the Hillel materials before us, but it will take much study before we can suggest concrete hypotheses about him.

The only firm conclusion is that Hillel was likely to have lived sometime before the destruction of the Temple and to have played an important part in the politics of the Pharisaic party. We may further hypothesize that traditions about his teachings on the festivals (Passover), on purity laws, and on legal theory (the ordinances) may go back to him. But the materials before us are so highly developed and sophisticated that we cannot recover anything like his words.

CONCLUSION

If you go to an art museum and see pictures of biblical scenes as medieval and early modern painters imagine them, you notice that the artists always take for granted that people long ago dressed and looked the way the artists' contemporaries did in their own time. People quite naturally project backward, into remote antiquity, the customs and habits of their own day. That is so not only visually, but also conceptually, intellectually. The reason is that, until the nineteenth century, people defined the issues of the past differently from the way they then began to. They took for granted that what had happened long ago was important because of the lessons, pertinent to contemporaries, taught by history. They looked for proofs for disputed propositions of the day, to be derived from the authority of the ancients. Accordingly, people recognized no space in the time between themselves and the past. The notion of anachronism—reading backward issues pertinent only later on—impressed no one. In the nineteenth century and afterward, minds changed. Perspectives shifted, so that people wanted to know not how the past was relevant, hence reshaped in the model of the present. They asked, rather, what had "really" happened. In our context, that meant to investigate not the Christ treasured by the church, but "the historical Jesus," as he "really" *was*. Among the treasures of the church, historians (who invariably were also theologians) purported to select the things Jesus had really said and to set aside those they regarded as "inauthentic."

Now if you reflect upon the rather alien and odd materials about Hillel, the one thing you will recognize is that they were made up or constructed for some purpose other than to preserve the very words Hillel had spoken, the very deeds he had done. The interest in Hillel always was to find in him a model for the time of the story-teller. If we ask not about the "historical Hillel" but about the Hillel of history, that is, about how Hillel lived on in the minds and imaginations of the great rabbis of Judaism, we get exact and reliable answers. Every story then is a fact. It testifies to what people later thought Hillel had said and done. It tells us, then, about the things rabbis maintained all Jews should say and do: the model of virtue, the mode of correct reasoning alike. Hillel then *is*: he endures. He never dies. He is the teacher, he is the paradigm. That is why the stories reach us. That, it seems to me, stands then for the purpose for which the stories were made up and preserved. They are documents of culture, glyphs of faith. If now you go back over the stories and ask the question I did not ask, namely, what in fact is the point of this story? you will find the answer right on the surface. It will lead you deep into the heart and mind of the religious world of Judaism.

Whether or not the issue of "the historical Jesus" runs parallel to the question of "the historical Hillel" remains for Christians to work out. Clearly, the claim that Jesus had said "this but not that" weighs in on the scales of theological debate. Assuredly, the treasure of faith that is the heritage of the church invariably imputes exact historical factuality to each and every story and saying. I wonder, however, whether in the context of faith—whether concerning Moses, Jesus, or Muhammad—such a thing as "critical history" in the nineteenth-century sense indeed can emerge. I ask myself whether, to begin with, the sources came into being with any such purpose in mind. And I question whether, when we ask about history in the narrow sense at hand, we address the right questions to sources of such a character. And, anyhow, what "critical historical" facts can ever testify to the truth or falsity of salvation, holiness, joy, and love?

The Destruction
of the Temple
and the Renaissance
of Torah

5

JUDAISM
BEYOND
CATASTROPHE

To understand the context in which the first Christians in the Land of Israel received Christ and responded to his life and teachings, we have to return one last time to the destruction of Jerusalem and the cessation of the service of sacrifice to God at the Temple. The entire history of Christianity and Judaism alike flowed across the abyss of that catastrophe. Each religious tradition had to make sense of what it meant to worship God in ways lacking all precedent in the history of Israel, of which each religious tradition claimed to be the natural outcome and fulfillment. Accordingly, we return to the religious meaning of that awesome event, the end of a thousand-year-old cult and culture, the beginning of what we now know to be a two-thousand-year continuation, in old new ways, of ancient Israel's life in Judaism and Christianity. We review the meanings of the events of 70 C.E. as those events are portrayed in rabbinical writings of later times that refer to them: the theological issue, the rabbinical response. The principal figure at hand, Yohanan ben Zakkai, described in rabbinical writings as Hillel's leading disciple, is represented as the master, the sage and rabbi, whose teachings guided Israel beyond the end, so we focus upon stories and sayings told about and assigned to him. Yavneh was the town in which he had taken refuge.

THEOLOGICAL CHALLENGE

Yohanan ben Zakkai turned, first of all, to the problem of faith. At Yavneh his attention was drawn to the deep despair of the Jews. With Jerusalem in Roman hands and the Temple in ruins, some saw themselves as the rejected children of God, born to disaster. Others accepted the prophetic teaching that suffering was punishment for sin and reflected more thoughtfully on the nature of human transgression. They reconsidered ancient analyses of man's shortcoming in the light of the fresh catastrophe. Still others, both on the Roman and the Jewish sides as well as within the nascent Christian community, offered an explanation of the cataclysm in terms of their own understanding of human history. Most were obsessed with the recent unfortunate events. They wondered what to make of the national disaster. The result was preoccupation with the future and hope for quick recompense.

Yohanan differed from the rest of his generation. He concerned himself with the prevailing needs of the surviving remnant of Israel. While he shared the common sense of tragedy and endured the despair of his generation, he did not fix his vision on what had happened and what would come to compensate for the catastrophe. He instead attempted to devise a program for the survival and reconstruction of the Jewish people and faith. Thus, retrospectively, a paradox emerges. Out of preoccupation with the sufferings of the past came neurotic obsession with the secret of future redemption. From stubborn consideration of present and immediate difficulties came a healthy, practical plan by which Israel might in truth hold on to what could be saved from the disaster. Others offered the comfort that as certainly as punishment has followed sin, so surely would he who chastised the people comfort, then redeem them. Therefore Israel ought to wait for inexorable redemption. Yohanan, on the other hand, proposed a program and a policy for the interim during which the people had to wait.

The people had to be told, first of all, why they suffered. Romans and Jewish loyalists, Jewish Christians, Jewish apocalyptics, and Yohanan—all advanced answers to this question, agreeing that the sin of Israel had brought disaster, but disagreeing on precisely what that sin was. The obvious answer, given by the victorious party, was that Israel had sinned by relying on force of arms, by rebelling against Roman rule. Josephus in the *Wars* emphasized that the sins of the nation had guaranteed the Roman victory: "Invariably arms have been refused to our nation, and warfare has been the sure signal of defeat. For it is, I suppose, the duty of the occupants of holy ground to leave everything to the rule of God, and to scorn the aid of human hands, can they but conciliate the Arbiter above." Josephus was particularly concerned about driving home this point, because the Romans had hired him to write the book partly in order to dissuade the Jews of Mesopotamia and Babylonia from trying to secure

Parthian intervention in Palestine. The Romans likewise regarded the catastrophe as direct recompense for rebellion against Rome, a sin compounded by the sheer inconvenience of the war, coming when the imperial succession was in doubt, other lands in revolt, and the armies fighting a civil war. Josephus reported that Titus thus addressed the city:

> You without bestowing a thought on our strength or your own weakness have through inconsiderate fury and madness lost your people, your city, and your Temple.
> You were incited against the Romans by Roman humanity. . . . We allowed you to occupy this land, and set over you kings of your own blood; then we maintained the laws of your forefathers, and permitted you . . . to live as you willed.

Nonetheless, Israel had rebelled. Whose fault was it then that the Temple was destroyed? Israel sinned by the act of war and was punished by the conquest. In later decades even some Jews came to see matters in this way, but only after the utter devastation of vast territories in the Bar Kokba rebellion sixty-five years later.

The Christian Jews of Jerusalem had held the Temple sacred for thirty years, participating in its rites and frequenting its courts. After the destruction, the Christian community held that the final punishment had at last come on the people who had rejected Jesus Christ. The church naturally came to regard the catastrophe as a vindication of Christian faith. Eusebius preserved the Christian viewpoint:

> Those who believed in Christ migrated from Jerusalem, so when holy men had altogether deserted the royal capital of the Jews . . . the judgment of God might at last overtake them for all their crimes against Christ and his apostles, and all that generation of the wicked be utterly blotted out from among men. . . . Such was the reward of the iniquity of the Jews and of their impiety against the Christ of God.

The Christians thus thought that Jerusalem had suffered the punishment of its inhabitants, who had sinned against Christ.

The Jewish apocalyptics likewise blamed Israel's sins for the disaster, meditated on the nature of sin, and comforted the people with the promise of impending redemption, of which they declared, "Thrice blest the man who lives until that time." Two documents, the apocalypse of Ezra and the vision of Baruch, are representative of the apocalyptic state of mind. The author (or editor) of the Ezra apocalypse (II Ezra 3—14), who lived at the end of the first century

C.E., looked forward to a day of judgment when the Messiah would destroy Roman power, and the rule of God would govern society. He wondered at the same time how Israel's continued sufferings might be reconciled with divine justice. To Israel, God's will had been revealed, but God had not removed the evil inclination which prevented the people from carrying out that will: "For we and our fathers have passed out lives in ways that bring death. . . . But what is man, that thou art angry with him, or what is a corruptible race, that thou art so bitter against it?" (II Ezra 8:26) Ezra was told that God's ways are inscrutable (4:10–11), but when he repeated the question, "Why has Israel been given over to the gentiles as a reproach," he was given an answer characteristic of this literature. A new age is dawning which will shed light on such perplexities. The pseudepigraphic Ezra regarded the catastrophe as the fruit of sin, more specifically, the result of man's *natural* incapacity to do the will of God. He prayed for forgiveness and found hope in the coming transformation of the age and the promise of a new day, when man's heart will be as able, as his mind even then was willing, to do the will of God.

The pseudepigraph in the name of Jeremiah's secretary, Baruch, likewise brought promise of coming redemption, but with little practical advice for the intervening period. The document exhibited three major themes. First, God acted righteously in bringing about the punishment of Israel:

> Righteousness belongs to the Lord our God, but confusion of face to us and our fathers. . . . The Lord has brought them upon us, for the Lord is righteous in all his words (Baruch 2:6).

Second, the catastrophe came on account of Israel's sin:

> Why is it, O Israel . . . that you are in the land of your enemies? . . . You have forsaken the fountain of wisdom, if you had walked in the way of the Lord, you would be dwelling in peace forever (3:10).

Third, as surely as God had punished the people, so certainly would he bring the people home to their land and restore their fortunes. Thus Jerusalem speaks:

> But I, how can I help you? For He who brought these calamities upon you will deliver you from the hand of your enemies. . . . Take courage, my children, cry to God, and He will deliver you from the power and hand of the enemy. . . . For I sent you out with sorrow and weeping, but God will give you back to me with joy and gladness forever (4:17–18, 21, 23).

Finally, Baruch advised the people to wait patiently for redemption, saying:

> My children, endure with patience the wrath that has come upon you from God. Your enemy has overtaken you, but you will soon see their destruction and will tread upon their necks. . . . Take courage, my children, and cry to God, for you will be remembered by Him who brought this upon you. For just as you purposed to go astray from God, return with tenfold zeal to seek Him, for He who brought these calamities upon you will bring you everlasting joy with your salvation. Take courage, O Jerusalem, for He who named you will comfort you (4:25, 27–30).

This theme came very close to Yohanan's comments on the destruction, for Baruch emphasized, as did Yohanan, the comfort to be found in the very authorship of the calamity. Yohanan however emphasized the duty of the people to repent and return to God as the *condition* of redemption. Baruch regarded redemption as a present hope, which would be fulfilled in a short while, while Yohanan gave no indication except in his very last breath that he expected the redemption in the near future. So far as the consolation of Baruch depended on immediate redemption, it thus was not consonant with the opinions of Yohanan ben Zakkai, who never said, "Endure with patience . . . because redemption is close at hand."

YOHANAN'S RESPONSE

Yohanan, always skeptical of messianic movements among the people, taught:

> If you have a sapling in your hand, and it is said to you, "Behold, there is the Messiah"—go on with your planting, and afterward go out and receive him. And if the youths say to you, "Let us go up and build the Temple," do not listen to them. But if the elders say to you, "Come, let us destroy the Temple," listen to them. The building of youth is destruction, and the destruction of old age is building—proof of the matter is Rehoboam, son of Solomon (Abot de Rabbi Nathan, Text B, Chap. 31).

Yohanan offered not hope of speedy redemption, but rather a conditional promise: just as punishment surely followed sin, so will redemption certainly follow *repentance*.

Yohanan had a detailed, practical program to offer for the repair of the Jewish soul and reconstruction of the social and political life of the Land of Israel. It was, first, to provide the people with a source of genuine comfort by showing them how they might extricate themselves from the consequences of their sins. Second, he placed new emphasis upon those means of serving the Creator which had survived the devastated sanctuary. Finally, he offered a comprehensive program for the religious life, a program capable of meeting this and any future vicissitude in Israel's history. By concentrating on the immediate problems of the day, Yohanan showed how to transcend history itself—not through eschatological vision, but through concrete actions in the workaday world. His message of comfort was preserved in this story:

> *Because thou didst not serve the Lord thy God with joyfulness and gladness of heart, by reason of the abundance of all things, therefore thou shalt serve thine enemies whom the Lord will send against thee in hunger and thirst, in nakedness and in want of all things* (Deut. 28:47–48).

Once Rabban Yohanan ben Zakkai was going up to Emmaus in Judea, and he saw a girl who was picking barleycorn out of the excrement of a horse.

Said Rabban Yohanan ben Zakkai to his disciples, "What is this girl?"

They said to him, "She is a Jewish girl."

"And to whom does the horse belong?"

"To an Arabian horseman," the disciples answered him.

Then said Rabban Yohanan ben Zakkai to his disciples, "All my life I have been reading the following verse, and I have not until now realized its full meaning: *If you do not know, O fairest among women, follow in the tracks of the flock, and pasture your kids beside the shepherds' tents* (Song of Songs 1:8).

"You were unwilling to be subject to God, behold now you are subjected to the most inferior of nations, the Arabs. You were unwilling to pay head-tax to God, *a beqa a head* [Exod. 38:26]. Now you are paying a head-tax of fifteen sheqels under a government of your enemies.

"You were unwilling to repair the roads and streets leading up to the Temple. Now you have to keep in repair the posts and stations on the road to the imperial cities. And thus it says, *Because thou didst not serve.* . . . Because you did not serve the Lord your God with love, therefore you shall serve your enemy with hatred. Because you did not serve the Lord your God when you had plenty, therefore you shall serve your enemy in hunger and thirst. Because you did not serve the Lord your God when you were well clothed, therefore you shall serve your enemy in nakedness. Because you did not serve the Lord your God by reason of the abundance of all things, therefore shall you serve your enemy in want of all things."

Yohanan thereupon exclaimed, "Happy are you, O Israel! When

you obey the will of God, then no nation or race can rule over you! But when you do not obey the will of God, you are handed over into the hands of every low-born people, and not only into the hands of the people but even into the power of the cattle of that low-born people" (Mekhilta de R. Ishmael, trans. Lauterbach, 2:193–4).

This incident epitomizes Yohanan's viewpoint on the disaster. He never said, "Take comfort because in a little while, suffering will cease." Yohanan called on the people to *achieve* a better fortune through their own efforts. Like Josephus, he taught that Israel can be happy if it submits to God and to the Romans and follows the laws laid down by both. Both conceived of the fulfillment of Jewish law as interpreted by the Pharisees to be the good life in this world and assurance of a portion in the next. Yohanan, unlike Josephus, did not go to Rome, but remained at home among the suffering folk.

In later years Rabbi 'Aqiba, believing that Ben Koziba (Bar Kokba) was the Messiah, became impatient with the results of Yohanan's limited program. He urged his followers to rebel once again. This act represented the failure of courage, the nerve to wait. Because the people had grown impatient with their own capacities, they looked to God for immediate deliverance. The consequence was a new revolution. Another rabbi rebuked 'Aqiba: "Grass will grow on your cheeks, 'Aqiba ben Joseph, but the Messiah will not have appeared." In the meantime, however, the nation was plunged once again into revolution and met a far greater disaster than before.

"FOR I DESIRE MERCY, NOT SACRIFICE"

Yohanan had earlier taught, in commenting on the words of Qohelet, "Let your garments always be white, and let not oil be lacking on your head" (Eccles. 9:8), that Jews should clothe themselves in Torah, commandments, and acts of kindness. Each of these categories represented a fundamental concern of the pious. Through the study of Torah, people learned what their God wanted of them. Through doing the commandments, they carried out that will. Through acts of lovingkindness they freely honored God who gave the Torah. These elements were probably a transformation of the teachings of Simeon the Righteous two centuries earlier: "On three things does the age stand: on the Torah, on the Temple service, and on acts of piety." By "Torah" Simeon had meant the books of the Torah; by "Temple service," the sacrificial cult in Jerusalem; by "acts of piety," acts of loyalty and obedience to God. Yohanan survived the destruction of the Temple. He came at the end of a long struggle for the Torah, both written and oral, as interpreted by the Pharisees. Acts of obedience to God seemed to him to comprehend a broader obligation than piety. He therefore infused these categories with new content. We here see his thought:

> Once as Rabban Yohanan ben Zakkai was coming out of Jerusalem, Rabbi Joshua followed him, and beheld the Temple in ruins.
> "Woe unto us," Rabbi Joshua cried, "that this place, the place where the iniquities of Israel were atoned for, is laid waste."
> "My son," Rabban Yohanan said to him, "be not grieved. We have another atonement as effective as this. And what is it? It is acts of lovingkindness, as it is said, *For I desire mercy, not sacrifice* [Hos. 6:6]" (Abot de Rabbi Nathan, trans. Goldin, 34).

Yohanan's treatment of the verse, "For I desire mercy, not sacrifice," was consistent with the contemporary hermeneutic. In biblical times, *hesed* had meant (in part) the mutual liability of those who are friends and relatives, master and servant, or any relationship of joint responsibility. In relationship to God *hesed* meant acts of conformity to the covenant between man and God. Hosea meant that God demanded loyal adherence to his covenant, rather than sacrifice. By Yohanan's time, however, the word had acquired a different connotation. It meant mercy or an act of compassion and lovingkindness. Thus to Jesus of Nazareth was attributed the saying: "Those who are well have no need of a physician, but those who are sick. Go and learn what this means, 'I desire mercy [eleon] and not sacrifice.' For I came not to call the righteous, but sinners" (Matt. 9:12–13). Later rabbinic sources likewise preserved this connotation in commenting on the verse. The verse was likewise understood in the *Recognitions of Clement*, in an exegesis strikingly similar to Yohanan's:

> This place which seemed chosen for a time, often harassed as it had been by hostile invasions and plunderings, was at last to be wholly destroyed. And in order to impress this upon them even before the coming of the true prophet, who was to reject at once the sacrifices and the place, it was often plundered by enemies and burnt with fire, and the people carried into captivity among foreign nations, and then brought back when they betook themselves to the mercy of God; that by these things they might be taught that a people who offer sacrifices are driven away and delivered up into the hands of the enemy, but they who do mercy and righteousness are without sacrifices freed from captivity and restored to their native land.

Yohanan thought that through *hesed* the Jews might make atonement, and that the sacrifices now demanded of them were love and mercy. His choice of the verse in Hosea gave stress to the ethical element of his earlier trilogy of the study of Torah, doing the commandments, and acts of lovingkindness. Yohanan emphasized the primacy of *hesed* itself in the redemptive process: *Just as the Jews needed a redemptive act of compassion from God, so must they now act compassionately in order to make themselves worthy of it.* This primary emphasis in personal moral quality rather than in specific external action, either ritual or legal, is in accordance with the increasing concern for the inner aspect of religion characteristic of the age. The act of compassionate fellowship, which in Yohanan's opinion was the foundation of true religion, became the central focus of his consoling message for the new and troubled age.

Yohanan shared the common sense of grief and taught, like others, that the sins of the nation had brought the disaster. But he added that its virtues might bring redemption. He differed from others in rejecting the eschatological focus of consolation. He offered the ideal of *hesed*, a means by which Jews might change their own hearts. He provided an interim ethic by which the people might live while they awaited the coming redemption. The earlier age had stood on the books of the Torah, the Temple rites, and acts of piety. The new age would endure on the foundation of studying the Torah, doing the commandments, and especially performing acts of compassion. Compassion strikingly embodied that very quality which the brutality of war must paradoxically have accentuated in his mind: humankind's capacity to act kindly and decently to fellow humans.

The consequence of Yohanan's lesson may have been embodied in a later encounter between his disciple Joshua and a group of apocalyptists. One recalls that 2 Baruch had lamented:

> Blessed is he who was not born, or he who having been born has died,
> But as for us who live, woe unto us. Because we see the afflictions of
>   Zion, and what has befallen Jerusalem . . .
> You husbandmen, sow not again. Jerusalem . . .
> You husbandmen, sow not again.
> And earth, why do you give your harvest fruits?
> Keep within yourself the sweets of your sustenance.
> And you, vine, why do you continue to give your wine?
> For an offering will not again be made therefrom in Zion,
> Nor will first-fruits again be offered.
> And do you, O heavens, withhold your dew,
> And open not the treasuries of rain.
> And do you, sun, withhold the light of your rays,
> And you moon, extinguish the multitude of your light.

For why should light rise again
Where the light of Zion is darkened?
Would that you had ears, O earth,
And that you had a heart, O dust,
That you might go and announce in Sheol,
And say to the dead,
"Blessed are you more than we who live."

(2 Baruch 10:6-7, 9-12; 11:6-7)

Yohanan's student Joshua met such people. It was reported that when the Temple was destroyed, ascetics who would not eat flesh or drink wine multiplied in Israel. Rabbi Joshua dealt with them:

He said to them, "My children, on what account do you not eat flesh and drink wine?"

They said to him, "Shall we eat meat, from which they used to offer a sacrifice on the altar, and now it is no more? And shall we drink wine, which was poured out on the altar, and now it is no more?"

He said to them, "If so, we ought not to eat bread, for there are no meal offerings any more. Perhaps we ought not to drink water, for the water offerings are not brought any more."

They were silent.

He said to them, "My children, come and I shall teach you. Not to mourn at all is impossible, for the evil decree has already come upon us. But to mourn too much is also impossible, for one may not promulgate a decree for the community unless most of the community can endure it. . . . But thus have the sages taught: 'A man plasters his house, but leaves a little piece untouched. A man prepares all the needs of the meal, but leaves out some morsel. A woman prepares all her cosmetics, but leaves off some small item'" (Babylonian Talmud Baba Batra 60b).

CONCLUSION

If we appreciate the force of powerful emotions aroused by the Temple cult, we may understand how grand a revolution was effected in the simple declaration, so long in coming, that with the destruction of the Temple the realm of the sacred had finally overspread the world. We must now see in ourselves, in our selfish motives to be immolated, the noblest sacrifice of all. So Rabban Gamaliel son of Rabbi Judah the Patriarch said, "Do His will as if it was your will, so that He may do your will as if it was His will. Make your will of no effect before His will, that He may make the will of others of no effect before your will." His will is that we love our neighbors as ourselves. Just as willingly as we would contribute bricks and mortar for the building of a sanctuary, so willingly we ought to contribute love, renunciation, self-sacrifice, for the building of a sacred community. If one wants to do something for God in a time when the Temple is no more, the offering must be the gift of selfless compassion. The holy altar must be the streets and market-places of the world.

A
FINAL
WORD

The ancient rabbis look out upon a world destroyed and still smoking in the aftermath of calamity, but they speak of rebirth and renewal. The holy Temple lay in ruins, but they ask about sanctification. The old history was over, but they look forward to future history. Theirs, as we see, is a message that what is true and real is the opposite of what people perceive. God stands for paradox. Strength comes through weakness, salvation through acceptance and obedience, sanctification through the ordinary and profane, which can be made holy. Now to informed Christians, the mode of thought must prove remarkably familiar. For the cross that stands for weakness yields salvation, and the crucified criminal is king and savior. That is the foolishness to which the apostle Paul makes reference. Yet the greater the "nonsense"—life out of the grave, eternity from death—the deeper the truth, the richer the paradox! So here we have these old Jews, one group speaking of sanctification of Israel, the people, the other of salvation of Israel and the world. Separately, they are thinking along the same lines, coming to conclusions remarkably congruent to one another, affirming the paradox of God in the world, of humanity in God's image, in the rabbinical framework; of God in the flesh, in the Christian. Is it not time for the joint heirs of ancient Israel's Scripture and hope to meet once more, in humility, before the living God? Along with all humanity, facing backward toward Auschwitz and total destruction, and forward toward complete annihilation of the world as we know it—is it not time?

FOR
FURTHER
READING

FOR CHAPTER 1

Historical background and bibliography

Schuerer, Emil. *The History of the Jewish People in the Age of Jesus Christ (175 B.C.–A.D. 135).* 2 vols. A New English Version. Revised and edited by Geza Vermes and Fergus Millar. Literary Editor, Pamela Vermes. Organizing Editor, Matthew Black. Edinburgh: T. & T. Clark, 1973–1979.
This magisterial work brings up to date the classic scholarly account of the subject. Vermes and Millar have revised and reworked every chapter. From their account and the bibliographies they provide, the student can pursue virtually any imaginable topic in the study of the context, in Judaism, in which Christianity was born.

FOR CHAPTER 2

Religion

Moore, George F. *Judaism: The Age of the Tannaim.* Cambridge, Mass.: Harvard University Press, 1954.
Neusner, Jacob. *Judaism: The Evidence of the Mishnah.* Chicago: University of Chicago Press, 1981.
———. *Judaism: The Evidence of the Yerushalmi.* Chicago: University of Chicago Press, 1983.
For the study of all forms of Judaism other than that called "rabbinic," "talmudic," or "classical," Schuerer-Vermes-Millar must be regarded as the primary introduction. The Judaism revealed in the canon of rabbinical literature is systematically described in the books listed above.
Urbach, Ephraim E. *The Sages: Their Concepts and Beliefs.* Jerusalem: The Magnes Press, 1975.

Literature

Neusner, Jacob, *The Study of Ancient Judaism.* Vol. 1, *Mishnah, Midrash, Siddur.* Vol. 2, *The Palestinian and Babylonian Talmuds.* New York: KTAV Publishing House, 1981.

> The essays collected in these books provide bibliographical introductions to the principal components of the rabbinical canon. An English translation of the update of the German classic on rabbinical literature by H. L. Strack, revised and amplified by Guenther Stemberger, will be published by KTAV Publishing House some time in the mid-1980s. For those who can read German, the new edition is compendious and valuable: Strack, Hermann L. and Stemberger, Guenther. *Einleitung in Talmud und Midrasch.* 7th ed., rev. and expanded. Munich: Verlag C. H. Beck, 1982.

FOR CHAPTERS 3 AND 4

The Pharisees and Hillel

Finkelstein, Louis. *The Pharisees: The Sociological Background of Their Faith.* Philadelphia: Jewish Publication Society of America, 1946.

Marcus, Ralph. "The Pharisees in the Light of Modern Scholarship," *Journal of Religion* 23 (1952):153–64.

Neusner, Jacob. *The Rabbinic Traditions About the Pharisees Before 70.* 3 vols. Leiden: E. J. Brill, 1971.

Rivkin, Ellis. *A Hidden Revolution: The Pharisees' Search for the Kingdom Within.* Nashville: Abingdon Press, 1978.

> Readers will be astonished at the different pictures of the Pharisees presented in the books listed above. In chapter 3 of this book I have provided as conventional an account of the problem as I am able. Then in chapter 4 I provide a picture of the way in which I think the sources are to be read. That way is markedly different from the manner in which, among others, Moore, Finkelstein, and Rivkin make use of the same sources, and the difference in method accounts for the diversity of results. Students of the New Testament, used to the critical-historical method of analyzing texts for historical purposes, will find themselves at home in my approaches.

FOR CHAPTER 5

The Destruction of the Temple and Its Aftermath

Davies, W. D. *The Setting of the Sermon on the Mount.* New York and Cambridge: Cambridge University Press, 1964.

Smallwood, Mary. *The Jews Under Roman Rule.* Leiden: E. J. Brill. 1981.[2]

Neusner, Jacob. *A Life of Yohanan ben Zakkai.* 2d. ed., rev. Leiden: E. J. Brill, 1970.

————. *Development of a Legend: Studies on the Traditions Concerning Yohanan ben Zakkai.* Leiden: E. J. Brill, 1970.
Each book listed in this brief bibliography contains substantial bibliographies on all topics under discussion. We deal with the most-studied chapter in the history of the Jews and of Judaism, as well as in the history of Christianity.

FOR THE FORMATIVE PERIOD IN
THE HISTORY OF JUDAISM

Neusner, Jacob. *The Foundations of Judaism: Method, Teleology, Doctrine.* Philadelphia: Fortress Press, 1983–1985. I. *Midrash in Context: Exegesis in Formative Judaism.* II. *Messiah in Context: Israel's History and Destiny in Formative Judaism.* III. *Torah: From Scroll to Symbol in Formative Judaism.*

GLOSSARY

66–70 C.E. The first Jewish war against Rome began in 66 C.E. Jerusalem fell in August 70. The resistance continued in wilderness regions until 73. The dates given here generally stand for the period in which the war was fought.

70 C.E. The date of the destruction of the Temple in Jerusalem.

132–135 C.E. These are the generally accepted dates in which the second Jewish war against Rome was fought. Led by Bar Kokba, the war probably began in 132 and ended in 135.

Babylonian Talmud A systematic commentary and exegesis of thirty-seven of the sixty-three tractates of the Mishnah (see Mishnah), in which Jewish sages living in Babylonia explain the meaning of the Mishnah's rules.

Bar Kokba War The Second Jewish war against Rome. See 132–135 C.E.

Essenes A Jewish sect that lived by itself near the Dead Sea in the last centuries B.C.E. The sect stressed rules of purity and waited for a holy war to mark the end of time and the salvation of Israel.

gezerah shavah An argument constructed on the basis of the appearance of the same word or grammatical construction in two distinct phrases, in which case the rule governing the one applies also to the other.

haburah An association of especially pious Jews, in the early centuries C.E., who ate their meals in accord with the rules governing the priests' meals in the Temple.

Hasmonean Monarchs These are the Maccabees who rebelled against the Syrians in ca. 165 B.C.E. and who set up an independent Jewish state in the Land of Israel that lasted until ca. 50 B.C.E.

heqqesh An argument by analogy. Because of the presumed likeness of two distinct phrases, the same rule governing the one applied also to the other, as at *gezerah shavah*, given above.

hesed The Hebrew word understood in the times of the Mishnah and the Talmud to mean "lovingkindness."

GLOSSARY

Josephus A Jewish general in the first war against Rome, who defected to the Romans and after the war wrote an account first of the war itself and second of the history of the Jews from biblical times to the end of the first century C.E.

Judah the Patriarch The ruler of the Jewish nation in the Land of Israel from the last part of the second century to the first part of the third, who promulgated the Mishnah. See Mishnah.

Mishnah A systematic law code covering the ways in which the important aspects of Jewish life might be sanctified in accord with God's will, with special attention to economic, social, family, civil, and cultic life. The basic document, after the Hebrew Bible, of Judaism. Completed in the late second century C.E.

Nasi The Hebrew word for "patriarch" or ruler. The title was given to Judah, ruler of the Jews when the Mishnah was put into effect, and is translated as Judah the Patriarch.

Oral Torah When God revealed the Torah (=God's will) to Israel at Mount Sinai, rabbinic Judaism maintains God gave revelation, or Torah, in two media: one, in writing, as in the Scriptures; the second, orally, handed on through memorization and ultimately written down in the Mishnah and related writings.

Palestinian Talmud A systematic exegesis of thirty-nine of the sixty-three tractates of the Mishnah, produced in the Land of Israel ("Palestine") around 400 C.E.

Philo A Jewish philosopher who lived in Alexandria at the turn of the first century C.E.

qal vehomer An argument a fortiori: if the rule applies in an unimportant case, it will all the more so apply in an important one.

Qohelet The Hebrew word for the biblical book of Ecclesiastes.

Qumran The location, in modern times, in which the Essene library near the Dead Sea was unearthed.

shekinah The Hebrew word for the Presence of God in the world.

Tosefta A collection of teachings that supplement the statements of the Mishnah's authorities, by expanding on them or giving parallel versions of sayings to those presented in the Mishnah.

Written Torah The Hebrew Scriptures revealed by God to Moses at Mount Sinai, as distinct from the Oral Torah. See Oral Torah.

Yavneh The town on the coast of the Land of Israel, well south of present-day Tel Aviv, at which Jewish sages took refuge during the first war against Rome in 66–70 C.E. It was the center of the sages' government after the war, and the place in which Yohanan ben Zakkai, leader of the post-70 sages, spent his last years.

INDEX

BIBLICAL AND TALMUDIC REFERENCES

SUBJECTS

DATE DUE